The
Meditation
Bible

The
Meditation
Bible

The definitive guide to meditation

Madonna Gauding

 A GODSFIELD BOOK

An Hachette UK Company
www.hachette.co.uk

First published in Great Britain in 2005 by Godsfield Press,
a division of Octopus Publishing Group Ltd
2–4 Heron Quays
London E14 4JP
www.octopusbooks.co.uk

This edition published in 2009

ISBN: 978-1-84181-366-0

Printed and bound in China

2 4 6 8 10 9 7 5 3 1

Contents

PART 1

BEFORE YOU BEGIN

INTRODUCTION

If you are new to meditation, you will feel comfortable here. And if you are an experienced meditator, you may find renewed inspiration. Whether you are a beginner or have been meditating for some time, this book offers you a broad collection of simple, effective meditations for enriching your daily life and deepening your spiritual practice. All are clearly explained, with easy-to-follow instructions.

For each entry, you will find a short explanation and its unique benefits in bullet form. Below that you will find a paragraph or two with further information followed by a shaded box with clear, step-by-step instructions

on how to do the meditation including the best time to practise, and how to prepare.

The book is organized according to how the meditations can help you. For example, meditations for calming and centring feature in the first section. These practices lower your stress levels and help you feel balanced and centred in your body and mind. If you have a tough day at work or you are simply feeling overwhelmed by your kids, your spouse and

endless lists of things to do, these meditations
will help you calm down and return to sanity.
But before you start, you will be introduced to
basic breath meditation, the original meditation
taught by the Buddha 2,500 years ago. This
ancient form of meditation is a great starting
point if you are new to meditation. Because
breath meditation is so powerful and effective,
it is the basis for many of the other meditations
collected here.

Meditations for living mindfully follow the
introduction. If you are feeling distracted and
out of touch, if you are doing too many things
at once, these meditations will help you be more
mindful of what you are doing, and thinking. A
meditation on doing the dishes will teach you
how to be mindful of every aspect of a task. You
will learn that slowing down and practising
mindfulness will enrich your life and ultimately
makes you more productive.

Meditation is a very powerful tool for healing
body, mind and spirit and this aspect is featured next. Here you will learn to
use the power of visualization to promote healing and prevent illness. If you
struggle with addictions, if you have unhealed childhood trauma or you suffer

from depression, you will find a great variety of meditations to help you on your healing journey. Try meditating on a great old tree to regain your physical health after illness, or try visualizing the female Buddha Tara as she heals your fears and grants you longevity.

You will discover that meditation is not just sitting on a cushion – you can meditate on the move. Try walking a labyrinth, whirling like a Dervish or sweeping your floor as meditative practice. You will learn how to turn anything you do into a meditation for improving your life and deepening your spirituality. If you are a couch potato this section is for you.

We all want to be loving and compassionate, but it takes effort and practise. Meditations for love and compassion bring these concepts into your consciousness and help you to manifest them in your daily life. Learn the very powerful and beautiful Tibetan Buddhist practice of *tonglen* for generating love and compassion for yourself and others. You will find meditations on overcoming prejudice, understanding true love and exploring your heart *chakra*.

If you are in debt, if you need help but have trouble asking for assistance or you are faced with an ethical dilemma, let the problem-solving meditations support you in facing your difficulties. When you feel your problems are insurmountable, meditation can help you overcome your anxiety and discover creative, effective ways to remedy your situation.

Meditations for manifesting your dreams are explored. Through focused attention and visualization, you can engage your mind and heart in creating the life you want. You may want to clear out your past to make room for the new; you may visualize clearly the work you would like to do or manifest your dreams for the benefit of every one on the planet. You will learn that meditation can be a powerful tool for making your dreams come true.

Connecting to the Divine through meditation completes our exploration of this ancient practice. Meditations inspired by a variety of spiritual traditions, both Eastern and Western, help you to experience the Sacred. There is no requirement for faith or belief. Let these meditations introduce you to or deepen your own notion of something or some being, greater than yourself. Taste your own potential for spiritual growth.

WHAT IS MEDITATION?

You may think that meditation is an exotic practice connected with Eastern religions. Or you may think it has to do with a special sitting posture, requiring your legs to be folded pretzel-like and your hands arranged in strange ways. You may think it has to do with being 'holy'. Fortunately, none of the above is true.

Meditation is simply making a choice to focus your mind on something. In fact, reading a book is a form of meditation, as is watching a movie or advertising on TV. Thinking about your argument with your spouse this morning and the pile of work awaiting you at the office as you drive to work is meditation. Listening to a CD is meditation. Focusing carefully on which bunch of bananas to buy is a form of meditation.

Your mind and your external reality are in a constant state of flux. Every second of your life you are creating or constructing your reality through what you think about and what you take in from your environment. Over time you develop habits regarding what you think as well as habits regarding what you take in. For example, you may find that you are a worrier and like to watch violent crime programmes on TV. You may find that you fantasize about what you would like your life to be and read romantic novels on a daily basis. Since you are meditating all the time, the question is, 'what are you choosing to meditate on?'.

Many spiritual traditions utilize this tendency of human beings – always to be thinking, taking in information and creating experiences – to help create better lives. As long as you are always thinking, they conclude, why not consciously focus your mind on positive and beneficial subjects? Why not use meditation to learn how your mind and emotions work and develop positive habits of mind, body and spirit? In this way you can develop your potential as a human being – mentally, physically and spiritually.

Practise for a happier life

Meditation is not mystical, otherworldly or inaccessible. It is not reserved for the 'elite' nor those steeped in knowledge of Eastern or alternative religions. Meditation is very down-to-earth and practical and it is available to everyone regardless of what religion you currently practise. Although many of the meditations are inspired by ancient and modern spiritual traditions, none requires faith or belief. If you have no spiritual practice, or do not believe in a god or higher power, try these meditations with the motivation of simply creating a happier life for yourself.

You can meditate by simply creating special time consciously to focus your mind in positive and helpful ways, but it helps to have some direction and guidance as to how to do this. After trying out some of the meditation techniques found here, you will discover what feels right for you; from this you can create an ongoing meditation practice of your own. If you want to learn more, find a meditation teacher who will help you deepen and strengthen your practice. A teacher will often have a group of students associated with his or her practice. Besides having ongoing meditation instruction, you will have the support and companionship of your fellow students.

This book provides a variety of meditations to get you started. It also introduces a variety of meditation techniques. Try to be aware of which techniques you are using and how they work for you. You may find you are more comfortable with some and less with others. Or you may like to use a variety of techniques in your ongoing meditation practice. The techniques fall into four basic categories.

Focusing

In the first meditation technique, you focus your mind on an object. That object can be something external – a candle, an image of a Buddha or a picture of Christ, a flower – or an internal object such as your breath or heartbeat. The purpose of this technique is to quiet your mind of its constant thinking and attain a measure of peace. Focusing on an object helps you calm and centre yourself and stabilizes your mind. As a side benefit, because you will find it difficult to stop thinking totally, you will observe patterns in your thinking and your emotions, which will help you learn more about yourself. Focusing during meditation helps you focus on whatever you want in the rest of your life. It helps ready your mind for other forms of meditation.

Thinking

Instead of avoiding thought in order to calm, stabilize and focus your mind, in these meditations you think about a topic. You may be asked to think about a problem you are having, possibly some difficulty you have with anger. You might think about some virtue you want to develop, such as loving kindness or patience; or the fact that you and everything else in the universe is connected. You meditate on a topic by thinking about it in a focused way, with the intention of creating a positive change in yourself. In this way you train your mind to be more positive.

Visualizing

Many of the meditations will ask you to visualize something, to create a picture in your mind. Visualizing helps you create your reality, manifest your desires and intentions, change your behaviour and even alter your body processes. For example, in the Tara meditations you visualize a female Buddha who removes your fears and heals your illness. Visualizing is a very powerful tool in the meditator's tool kit. Don't worry if you feel you have a hard time seeing a picture in your mind's eye. With a little practise your visualizing skills will improve over time.

Experiencing

In some of the meditations you will be guided through a process and asked to experience whatever comes up for you. For instance, in one meditation you work with a partner and learn to remove barriers to your friendship and intimacy. In another, you are asked to experience your senses by focusing intensely on a piece of ripe fruit.

Each meditation will employ one or more of these techniques. It is important to remember that meditation techniques are a means to an end and not an end in themselves. They are not meant to foster competition or aggression. You may become very good at focusing your mind and be able to sit for hours with rock-solid focus on your breath. You may become a spiritual athlete of sorts. But if you don't use your ability to focus on becoming a positive, kinder, more compassionate person, then you will have missed the point.

So remember to set your motivation before you meditate. You might say: 'I would like to meditate today to help myself become a happier, kinder person so I may be of service to myself and others.' When you have completed your meditation, you might add: 'I dedicate my efforts for my highest benefit and for the highest benefit of all others.' These meditation 'bookends' will greatly enhance your meditation sessions.

WHY MEDITATE?

There is a reason why meditation has been practised in many cultures for thousands of years – because its benefits are almost too numerous to mention. In all areas – physical, mental, emotional, psychological and spiritual – meditation has the potential to ease your suffering and help you create a better life. But time is at a premium for most of us so you may ask 'is it really worth it for me to meditate?' The answer is a resounding 'yes'.

Meditate for better health

Simply meditating on your breath can lower your blood pressure, slow your heart rate and ease your anxiety. Meditation, as an adjunct to traditional or alternative medical treatment, can help you heal from various illnesses such as cancer and heart disease. It can help you manage pain and prevent illness by helping you to stay physically balanced and healthy. It creates contentment, peace and joy, which all help to ease your state of mind and in turn, help promote longevity.

Meditate to sharpen your mind

Start with the meditations in the first section, then use your sharpened and stabilized mind to enhance your meditations for healing, self-development and spiritual realization. You can bring your new-found mental skill and discipline to your work and

your family life, making you a more effective boss, worker, spouse, parent and friend. Being able to bring your full attention to a loved one or a child can do wonders for your relationships. Having the ability to focus and concentrate under heavy deadlines at work will make life easier for you and your co-workers.

Meditate to be more aware of your body and mind

Because you have so much stimulation from electronic media, over work, shopping and other entertainment, you may find you have trouble paying attention. Attention Deficit Disorder is on the rise with adults who live in fast-paced urban areas. If you feel overloaded you may 'shut down' as a way of coping with more than you can handle. As a result of multi-tasking and rushing all the time, you may find you are losing the ability to be mindful or fully aware. Try mindfulness meditation if you want to enliven your senses and enrich your life. Learn to live your life in the present and to appreciate the life that you have.

Meditate to balance your emotions

It is easy to develop a problem with anger because of a stressful life. Working long hours, with costs rising for everything, it is no wonder you feel on edge and get angry at the drop of a hat. World upheaval and unrest can contaminate your life with fear. Or you may have a tendency to be jealous and resentful of the success of others. Meditate if you want to stay conscious of your emotions and monitor your emotional patterns. You may find that some of the meditations help you to transform negative emotions into positive ones. Having mental peace and less emotional reactivity are just two of the benefits of long-term meditation practice.

Meditate to heal psychological problems

If you have issues you cannot seem to overcome on your own, get professional help. If you want to speed your recovery, meditate to enhance your therapy. If you have addictions, unresolved grief, childhood neglect or trauma or other psychological issues, meditation is a wonderful way to support yourself during the healing process. It helps you to make friends with yourself and let go of self-hate. If you have problems with procrastination at work or relationship difficulties, meditation can help you to overcome these. Let meditation be a great companion on your healing journey, helping you to take responsibility for your own recovery.

Meditate to contemplate the mysteries of life

If you feel bogged down in the materialistic view of the world that pervades our culture, meditate to transform and transcend it. Meditate if you want to understand the meaning of your life, your destiny, your connectedness to all living beings and the sacredness of reality. Spirituality is an overused word, but its root is 'spirit' and refers to the life-force and intelligent energy that pervades the Universe. You can call that force God, Buddha, Christ, Spider Woman or your higher power. Or you can simply be open to the idea that there is more to life than meets the eye. Meditate if you want to access that enlightened mind, so that perhaps you may one day become enlightened yourself.

PREPARATION

You will find that each meditation entry in this book suggests ways to prepare for that particular meditation. However, there are a few things you can do, in general, to prepare yourself for meditation practice.

First among these is to have an open mind. If you are new to meditation, you may find your views challenged by some of the exercises. If you are an experienced meditator, you may find the meditations are different from those you are used to practising.

There is an old Buddhist story called 'The Three Pots' that summarizes mental states that may hinder you in having an open mind. You must make sure that your pot (your mind) doesn't have holes in it, because the information will pass through without you digesting it and making it your own. Likewise, you don't want your pot to be upside down (or have a closed mind about meditation), because then nothing can get in. And, finally, you don't want a dirty pot contaminated by preconceived ideas. So the moral of the story is obvious. Whether you are a new meditator or an old hand, prepare yourself by having an open mind and being open to new experiences.

Be willing to let meditation change you. Even if it is positive, change can be scary. For example, if you meditate on love and compassion and your heart opens, you may find you feel more and are more sensitive to the pain of others. At first you may be uncomfortable but you will soon discover that having an open heart is less painful than having a closed one. If you meditate to subdue your anger and find that you have become more patient and tolerant of others, you may have to let go of the old angry self that is a big part of your protection and your identity. But the benefits will far outweigh your temporary discomfort that comes with change.

Prepare your body to make meditation physically easier. Many of the meditations suggest sitting in the traditional cross-legged posture. If you can't sit cross-legged you can always sit on a chair. But if you want to sit in the traditional way, you may want to prepare yourself with stretching exercises to increase your flexibility. Try the exercise routine outlined in the box on page 24.

Pre-meditation stretches

1 Sit on the floor with your legs extended in front of you. Bending from your waist, try to touch your toes. If you can't reach them stretch as far as you can. Don't bounce. Reach slowly forward and release. Repeat five times.

2 Move your extended legs apart into a 'V', as wide as is comfortable for you. Reach both hands towards the toes on your left foot then towards your right. Stretch gently, repeating five times on each side.

3 With soles touching, bring both feet towards you as close as you can. Your knees will be off the floor. While holding both feet together, gently push down on your knees with your elbows. Repeat slowly five times.

4 When you finish stretching, massage your legs thoroughly to improve circulation. Spend extra time massaging your feet and knees. Practising this short routine on a daily basis will improve your flexibility over time.

Yoga

One of the best companion practices for meditation, yoga can help stretch and lengthen your entire body, making sitting in meditation much easier. If possible sign up for a class and learn basic poses that you can do at home.

Use relaxation exercises to make the transition from your daily life to your meditation session. Even if you choose to meditate in the morning, you may need to make a conscious separation from the alarm clock, breakfast-making, dressing and getting ready for work routine. If you meditate in the evening, it is especially important to make the transition from work to meditation an easier one. It doesn't have to take long. Take just a few minutes to relax; making the transition will help your meditation to be more productive.

The corpse

One of the best relaxation exercises is the yoga posture called the 'corpse pose' or *savasana*.

1 Stretch out on a mat on the floor. Rest your hands, palms upwards, slightly extended from your sides. If it is a bit chilly in the room, cover yourself with a light blanket.

2 Consciously relax every muscle in your body starting with your toes. When you reach the crown of your head, stay in *savasana* for a few minutes longer.

3 When you are ready, slowly get up and move to your meditation spot and begin your meditation.

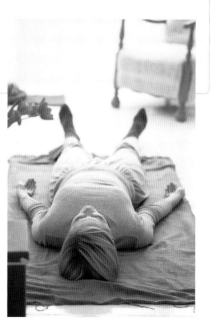

A great way to relax after work is to listen to calming music. Put on a CD of classical or 'new age' music that you find soothing and comforting. Listen to one or two tracks with your eyes closed. Let the day's stresses recede. When you are ready, move to your meditation cushion and begin your meditation.

WHAT YOU WILL NEED

Although not absolutely necessary, there are a few supplies you may want have on hand to make your meditation sessions more comfortable and productive. Most can be found online or in speciality shops or bookstores that carry meditation supplies. You might also try Buddhist or other meditation centres in your community. They often sell meditation supplies to their members and the general public.

Cushion or chair?

Since it is often recommended that you sit to meditate, you might want to consider buying a cushion made especially for meditation. They come in all shapes, sizes and colours, stuffed with a variety of materials, including syrofoam beads and buckwheat shells. Some are even adjustable. It is best to try them out first, if you can, and see what feels best to you.

In addition to your meditation cushion, you may also want to buy smaller support cushions for placing under your knees or ankles if you have pain in those areas.

If you have trouble sitting in the traditional position on the

floor on a cushion, you can sit on any regular straight-backed chair. Recently, some companies have produced 'meditation chairs' that fall somewhere between a normal chair and a cushion. They are made low to the floor and offer back support. You can sit on them cross-legged if you choose.

Another popular device called a 'backjack' allows you to sit on the floor but with support for your back. Companies that make meditation supplies have created a variety of these back support devices. If you have back problems but still want to sit in the traditional style, you may want to explore purchasing one of these.

Mats

If you buy a meditation cushion, you may want to invest in a larger flat mat, often called a *zabuton* that goes under your cushion. This serves to raise the cushion a little higher off the ground and also protects your ankles. For relaxation and some meditation poses that require lying flat on the ground, you may want to buy a thin portable yoga mat available at most yoga schools.

Blankets and shawls

If you plan to do relaxation poses, you may want a light blanket to place over yourself to keep you warm. Likewise, if you find yourself sitting for longer periods of time or early in the morning when it might be a little chilly, it is nice to have a blanket or shawl to put around you.

Loose clothing

Try to wear loose clothing when meditating. Avoid wearing a belt, a watch with a tight wristband or any piece of clothing that is binding or restricting in any way. Baggy trousers or a pair of tracksuit bottoms are great and a long loose skirt or caftan will work as well. Some companies make clothing especially for yoga and meditation, and you can find them online.

Prayer beads

Some of the meditations in this book suggest the use of prayer beads. Prayer beads are found in many spiritual traditions and in many cultures around the world. They are used to count the number of times you recite a prayer or mantra. They help connect your physical body to your mind while you are using mantra or prayer recitation as part of your meditation.

Buddhist prayer beads are the easiest to find online or in meditation centres. They come in a huge variety of colours and materials, and most have 108 beads. If you don't want a traditional one, you can find prayer beads that look like a bracelet which you wear on your wrist when not in use.

Bells, *tingshas* and singing bowls

Creating rituals will help you to maintain your practice over time. Beginning and ending your meditation with the sound of a bell or tiny cymbals called *tingshas* will help you focus and get the most out of your session. Singing bowls are actually a form of bell used

by Tibetan Buddhist practitioners. They can be from a few centimetres across to quite large in size. You ring or play them by rubbing a mallet around the rim, making a wonderful resonating sound. An ordinary bell works just as well to begin and end your sessions.

Timers

Some people find the use of timers too distracting. But if you want to time your meditation, you can use your watch placed within view on the floor in front of you. Or use any clock or kitchen timer. Using a timer in the beginning will help you become accustomed to what a ten- or twenty-minute session feels like.

CONSISTENCY

In order to reap the benefits of meditation, it is important to develop a consistent practice, daily if possible. The ritual of sitting down at the same time and in the same place every day will help make meditation a part of your life, like brushing your teeth or showering in the morning.

In the beginning you may want to sample meditations from each of the eight sections within this book. You will notice that there are suggestions for meditating while driving or doing other daily tasks. While in the exploration stage, feel free to meditate at different times of the day. But try to meditate once a day, regardless of the time or place. After you have explored different forms of meditation, you may find one or two you want to stay with on a long-term basis. At this point, settle on a time and place that is consistent day to day.

The changes, realizations and benefits of meditation accumulate over time. There is no quick fix or instant enlightenment. That is not to say that meditation will not feel good right away. But the more important benefits take place in the long term. They may be subtle or so profound that you will have a hard time describing them.

In the beginning, you may have trouble staying with a daily discipline. You may try a few meditations and then get distracted with other things. You may want to meditate but life seems to get in your way. Given the usual demands of

work, home and family, you will have no lack of reasons not to meditate. This is why committing to a daily practice is the best way to approach meditation. Your consistency will sustain you through periods of laziness, busyness or unhappiness with the speed of your progress. Hanging in there will pay off over time. After a while you will find your daily practice comforting and enjoyable, and you wouldn't miss it for the world.

SACRED SPACE

Sacred space is a place where you can connect with a world beyond your ordinary, everyday life – a site for meditation, prayer and ritual. This can be a corner of your bedroom set aside for meditation or a special place you create temporarily. If you are lucky enough to have an extra room, make that into your meditation space. But even if you live in a tiny, one-room apartment or live out of your suitcase, you can create sacred space for meditation.

Decide where you would like your meditation space to be. You may need to rearrange your chosen room to accommodate a meditation corner. Decide if your space can be permanent or if it has to be temporary, created only when you meditate. You will need enough space to accommodate your cushion or chair and an altar if you choose to create one.

Thoroughly clean the space you have chosen. Vacuum and dust, and if you have floors you can scrub, do so. Cleaning not only creates a tidy space, it clears negative energy in yourself, as well as in your environment.

Arrange your cushion or chair where you would like it to be. Sit down and make sure you feel comfortable in that spot. Are there any draughts? Create privacy by shutting the door to the room, but if that is not possible, try sitting behind a folding screen. Make sure the lighting is pleasing, whether artificial or natural. If you have a

yoga mat, additional small cushions, a bell, *tingshas*, a timer or prayer beads, store them nearby on a low shelf where you can reach them easily. If you would like to use music in your meditation, place a CD player nearby.

Creating an altar

If you feel comfortable having an altar, make sure your space is large enough to accommodate it when placed in front of your chair or cushion. There is no 'right way' to create an altar, so consider the following as suggestions to get you started.

Begin by finding a small, low table. Cover it with a beautiful cloth or scarf. On your altar, arrange items that have meaning for you. You might include deity figures or images – the Buddha, Tara, Christ or the Virgin Mary –

33

photos of your spiritual teachers, a spiritual text that is inspiring to you or offerings such as flowers, water, incense, candles and fruit. You may want to include symbols of the natural world such as a crystal, a beautiful stone or a shell. Consider adding a little stand for holding a spiritual saying or proverb that you find inspiring for that day.

Make sure that the objects you choose inspire you, help release and create energy, centre you and stimulate your imagination. Let them be aids in helping you understand yourself, your universe and your spiritual life.

Your sacred space can take up an entire room or it can be temporary. It can be miniature and portable. If you travel for a living or if you want to meditate at work, you can create sacred space in those environments as well.

Purchase a light, inflatable meditation cushion to pack in your suitcase or briefcase. If you want an altar, you can create a small, miniaturized one. Since ancient times, people have made use of travelling altars. Archaeologists have unearthed them in the form of amulets, images of spiritual teachers or images of deities designed to be carried or worn. Create your own travelling altar by assembling a kit with a small, framed image of a deity or teacher, a small bowl to make a water offering and perhaps a candle and some incense. Make sure the objects you choose are right for you. Include a beautiful cloth to place under your sacred objects. With your inflatable cushion and your travelling altar, you are all set! If you have a very tiny living space, you could use this at home as well.

Remember, your sacred space is utterly personal and as you continue to meditate, it may evolve over time. By creating this space, you honour your intention to live mindfully and provide room for your personal and spiritual growth. You invite the Sacred into your life.

MEDITATION POSTURES

Although you can meditate in any position, your posture is important when you meditate. As meditation is concerned with taming, healing and awakening your mind – and because your mind and body are inextricably linked – your posture is of great importance. When you meditate, you will learn that your body and breath can be a great help to your mind.

As you will discover, meditation can be practised in a variety of postures including sitting, walking, reclining and while doing other activities. However, most of the meditations recommend sitting. The traditional meditation of the Buddha is the seven-point meditation posture.

It may be hard for beginners to get used to the classical seven-point posture, but the rewards after a few sessions with aching knees are tremendous; once you master it, you can meditate in that position for the rest of your life. Correct posture helps your mind find peace, strength and control. It benefits your physical body by bringing your energies and systems into balance. Traditional Buddhist teachings suggest that it is possible to meditate all day in a classical posture, which you might find impossible in ordinary positions.

The classical seven-point posture

1 Sit on your cushion, with your spine, from nape of your neck to the small of the back, as straight as possible. The cushion raises your bottom a little higher to force your knees closer to the floor and helps your back stay straight. Sit a little forward on your cushion.

2 Cross your legs with your right leg above your left leg. The backs of your feet sit flat on the tops of your thighs. Ideally, your two feet make a straight line.

3 Keep your shoulders even and relaxed. Try not to sit with one shoulder higher than the other.

4 Your chin should be parallel to the floor and tucked in slightly.

5 Your eyes should be relaxed, open and slightly lowered, looking at nothing in particular about a metre (three feet) in front of you.

6 Place your tongue against your palate. Your lips should be slightly parted and your teeth should be touching but not clenched. Breathe through your nose.

7 Hand position is not part of the seven-point posture, but traditionally your hands should be cradled palms up, one on top of the other, four fingers'-width below the navel (not resting on your legs or feet). Your elbows are held slightly out from your body. But you can simply rest your hands on your knees.

Although beginners tend to find it easier to meditate with their eyes closed, it is better to train yourself to meditate with your eyes open. Closed eyes encourage thoughts, daydreaming and distraction. Your meditation then becomes associated with an 'other' or inner world rather than a clearer, truer way of seeing this world.

Relaxation is important. But if you are like most people, your body carries a great residual load of tension. Unfortunately, the effort to sit in meditation posture may produce even more tension in your body. So in the beginning, be kind to yourself. Learn to notice where you are tense or in pain, and release it slowly by relaxing over time. Make adjustments with small micro movements. The most important part of the posture is keeping your spine straight. If you can't cross your legs in seven-point style, do the best you can or sit in a chair. Then try to introduce the rest of the points as explained on page 37.

If you find it is too difficult to sit up straight because of back pain or injury, by all means use a back support. If you are ill and can't get out of bed, it is fine to meditate while lying down. If sitting is too difficult for you in the beginning because you are too anxious and literally can't sit still, then meditate while walking or running until you begin to calm your mind.

If possible, do what you can to make a sitting posture work for you. Remember to try the stretching exercises outlined in the Preparation section (see page 24). Or take a yoga class to increase your flexibility and get to know your body better. Try to challenge yourself, but know your limits. If you are coming to meditation later in life, don't torture yourself into thinking you have to sit in the traditional posture. One of the goals of meditation is to become a kinder person, so be sure you extend that kindness to yourself.

PART 2

THE MEDITATION
DIRECTORY

HOW TO USE THE DIRECTORY

You have now arrived at the heart of this book – the meditations. Here you will find 153 meditations divided into eight sections:

• Meditations for calming and centring

• Meditations for living mindfully

• Meditations for healing body, mind and spirit

• Meditations for getting you moving

• Meditations for generating love and compassion

• Meditations for solving your problems

• Meditations for manifesting your dreams

• Meditations for connecting to the divine

Of course, you may have our own ideas about how to use this directory, but here are a few to get you started.

Regardless of which approach you take, make your first meditation 'Watching your breath' on pages 50–1. This is the base of many of the other meditations in the book and the first meditation taught in many meditation centres around the world. The Buddha taught this practice over 2,500 years ago and it is just as powerful and effective today as it was then. Try it for a few days and if possible for a week. Always do a few minutes of breath meditation before all other meditations to prepare your mind. Then explore other meditations following the suggestions on the next page.

One way to use the directory is to read through all the meditations and note the ones you would like to try. In this way you will get a feel for the meditations all at once and you will soak up a great deal of information about meditation, how it is done and how it can help you. In other words, you will get a broad view of the meditation landscape, before you 'dive in'.

Another way to approach the directory is to read the introductions for each section listed on page 42, then rank them in order of interest to you. Note if any are particularly appealing or unappealing. If unappealing, ask yourself why. If you have a negative reaction to Meditations for Generating Love and Compassion, ask yourself why this is so. Do you have a broken heart you'd rather not touch, or a fear of being more open, loving and compassionate, and being hurt by others as a result?

Similarly, if you have a positive response to a section, explore why you are drawn to it. Maybe you are ready to heal and are happy to make 'Meditations for Healing Body, Mind and Spirit', first on your list. After you have ranked them in order and explored any strong reactions, read the meditations in the section you marked first, and check off those you would like to try. Start with the one that appeals most and work through the others.

A third way to use the directory is to combine it with divination. Sit quietly for a few moments. Ask that you be given the best meditation for you, for this moment in time. Then open the book randomly. Practise the meditation that appears. Afterwards note if your random choice surprised you and if you found it helpful for what is going on in your life at that point. A fourth way to approach the directory is to work through the meditations one at a time.

A list of the meditation's unique benefits.

The best time to practise the meditation.

Advice on how to prepare.

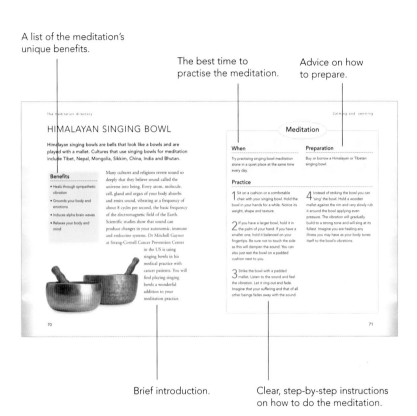

The meditation directory

Calming and centring

HIMALAYAN SINGING BOWL

Himalayan singing bowls are bells that look like a bowls and are played with a mallet. Cultures that use singing bowls for meditation include Tibet, Nepal, Mongolia, Sikkim, China, India and Bhutan.

Benefits

• Heals through sympathetic vibration

• Grounds your body and emotions

• Induces alpha brain waves

• Relaxes your body and mind

Many cultures and religions revere sound so deeply that they believe sound called the universe into being. Every atom, molecule, cell, gland and organ of your body absorbs and emits sound, vibrating at a frequency of about 8 cycles per second, the basic frequency of the electromagnetic field of the Earth. Scientific studies show that sound can produce changes in your autonomic, immune and endocrine systems. Dr Mitchell Gaynor at Strang-Cornell Cancer Prevention Center in the US is using singing bowls in his medical practice with cancer patients. You will find playing singing bowls a wonderful addition to your meditation practice.

Meditation

When

Try practising singing bowl meditation alone in a quiet place at the same time every day.

Preparation

Buy or borrow a Himalayan or Tibetan singing bowl.

Practice

1 Sit on a cushion or a comfortable chair with your singing bowl. Hold the bowl in your hands for a while. Notice its weight, shape and texture.

2 If you have a larger bowl, hold it in the palm of your hand. If you have a smaller one, hold it balanced on your fingertips. Be sure not to touch the side as this will dampen the sound. You can also just rest the bowl on a padded cushion next to you.

3 Strike the bowl with a padded mallet. Listen to the sound and feel the vibration. Let it ring out and fade. Imagine that your suffering and that of all other beings fades away with the sound.

4 Instead of striking the bowl you can 'sing' the bowl. Hold a wooden mallet against the rim and very slowly rub it around the bowl applying even pressure. The vibration will gradually build to a strong tone and will sing at its fullest. Imagine you are healing any illness you may have as your body tunes itself to the bowl's vibrations.

70

71

Brief introduction.

Clear, step-by-step instructions on how to do the meditation.

CALMING AND CENTRING

MEDITATIONS FOR CALMING AND CENTRING

Meditation helps you centre yourself in your body and calm your mind. You have probably seen pictures of people meditating, seated cross-legged on cushions, appearing serene and peaceful. Or perhaps you have admired a statue of the Buddha and noticed that he looked quite happy and at ease. You may find yourself drawn to meditation because you want to have that serenity in your own life.

The meditations in this first section will help you achieve the peace and calm you need to cope with a busy, fast-paced life. These are the first entries in the directory because you can best experience the meditations that follow if you approach them with a quiet and stabilized mind. 'Watching your breath' is perhaps the most important meditation in the directory and is the foundation for all the others. It may seem overly simple when you first try it; you may think it couldn't possibly help you. But give it time, at least a week, and you will begin to reap the benefits of this ancient and very effective meditation. It will help you reduce anxiety and mental chatter, lower your blood pressure and heart rate and help you focus and concentrate.

The other meditations in this section offer you a rich variety of exercises for attaining the serenity and peace you may be longing for. You will learn a great deal about your mind with 'Thought clouds', 'Spacious mind' and 'Distracted mind'. 'Nine-round breathing' will teach you a very powerful method to centre yourself before any activity, while 'Dancing flame' and 'Flowing water' make use of natural elements to quiet and calm your mind. 'Where is my mind now' will help you gain control of your thoughts. 'Sacred words', 'Gregorian chant' and 'Himalayan singing bowl' are wonderful meditations if you are aurally inclined. If you are a nature-lover, 'Star-gazing', 'Emotional mind', 'Mother Earth' and 'Flower power' all soothe and balance. 'Greet your day' and 'Tibetan sunset' will help you begin and end your day in a positive way. 'Centring prayer' helps you access your higher power. Create peace for yourself and others with 'Peace on Earth'. And if you have a particularly difficult crisis, 'Emotional storm' will help you through.

Before you try any of these meditations, set your intention to become a more calm and centred person. Try to bring peace and serenity into your daily life.

WATCHING YOUR BREATH

This is one of the simplest of all meditations, yet one of the most powerful and rewarding. Meditating on the breath on a daily basis provides a solid foundation for all other forms of meditation.

Benefits

- Reduces anxiety
- Lowers blood pressure and heart rate
- Reduces mental chatter
- Promotes ability to focus the mind
- Helps you concentrate on whatever you choose

The practice of meditating on the breath is thousands of years old. Ancient Hindus and Buddhists meditated in this way to tame uncontrolled thinking, reduce negative thoughts and actions, and gain an understanding of spiritual truths. Basically, you meditate on your breath in order to give your mind something to 'hang on to' when it starts to jump from one thought to another. Training your mind in this way helps you focus on one thing at a time, and develops your powers of concentration. It has a calming influence on your body and mind and is beneficial for reducing anxiety, lowering heart rate and blood pressure. Whether your interest is in spiritual development or mental and physical health, breath meditation is one the best all-round meditation practices.

Meditation

When

Meditate daily, morning and evening, for ten minutes. Build up to longer sessions.

Preparation

Find a quiet place at home where you will be undisturbed. You will need a cushion or a straight-backed chair. Wear loose-fitting, comfortable clothing. Create soft lighting and keep the room draught-free and at a comfortable temperature.

Practice

1 Sit cross-legged on a cushion with your bottom slightly raised. If you can't sit cross-legged, sit on a chair. Keep your back straight, your shoulders level and relaxed and your chin parallel to the floor. Lower your eyes and focus about a metre (three feet) in front of you. Rest your hands gently on your knees.

2 Breathe normally through your nose, using your abdomen rather than your chest. Check your posture and relax any part of your body that is tense.

3 Begin counting your breath on each exhalation; when you reach ten, begin again. Thoughts will intervene and when they do, simply let them go and return to counting your breath.

4 After ten minutes or so, end your session. Try to bring focus and concentration into your daily life.

THOUGHT CLOUDS

Thoughts inevitably arise when you meditate on your breath. Labelling your thoughts as they emerge will help you to refocus on your breath and calm your mind.

Benefits

- Helps calm your mind
- Gives perspective on thoughts
- Helps you be more flexible and open

It is normal to give your thoughts importance and equate them with 'truth' or 'reality'. Yet, one day you may think a person is your enemy – full of faults and evil motivations – and a month later you may have changed your opinion and now consider them a good friend. Through meditation you will begin to experience thoughts as ephemeral and changeable, like clouds moving across the sky. You will learn to loosen your grip on your thoughts and become more flexible and open. When thoughts emerge in your meditation, label them as 'thinking' and return your focus to your breath.

Meditation

When

Try this variation on breath meditation for ten minutes, morning and evening.

Preparation

Find a quiet place where you will be undisturbed. Before you begin to meditate notice how your mind moves continuously from one thought to another while in its ordinary state.

Practice

1 Sit cross-legged on a cushion with your bottom slightly raised. If you can't sit cross-legged, sit on a chair. Keep your back straight, your shoulders level and relaxed and your chin parallel to the floor. Lower your eyes and focus about a metre (three feet) in front of you. Rest your hands gently on your knees.

2 Breathe normally through your nose, using your abdomen rather than your chest. Check your posture and relax any part of your body that is tense.

3 Begin counting your breath and when you reach ten begin again. When thoughts intervene label them as 'thinking' and return to your breath.

4 Meditate in this way for about ten minutes. Try this meditation for a week. See if you notice how changeable and ephemeral your thoughts are.

SPACIOUS MIND

With one thought constantly following another, your mind may start to feel claustrophobic. This meditation will help you clear your mental 'space' and give you a much-needed mental holiday.

Benefits

- Gives your mind a rest from over-thinking
- Helps you feel more calm and compassionate
- Provides mental spaciousness

Our minds are filled with memories, desires, plans, worries and other mental impressions. Our constant thinking adds to the disarray. This meditation will help you clear your mental clutter and create a peaceful, open, spacious mind. By creating mental spaciousness, you will realize that you have much more control over how you feel and think than you imagined. You will discover your thoughts and problems take a back seat as you experience a reality that is larger and more compassionate than your ordinary mind. With practise you can experience this mental spaciousness whenever and wherever you want.

Meditation

When

Any time you are feeling stressed and hemmed in by worries or constant thinking, use this meditation.

Preparation

Before meditating, relax by stretching out on your bed or on the floor. Starting at your toes, move up your body and relax all of your muscles. Rest and breathe deeply for five breaths. Get up slowly and begin the meditation.

Practice

1 Sit crossed-legged on a cushion or a straight-backed chair with your feet flat on the floor.

2 Begin by focusing on your breath, counting on the out-breath up to ten. After about five minutes, stop counting your breath and simply focus on the out-breath for another two minutes or so.

3 Become aware of the calmness and space that arises at the end of the out-breath. Let yourself float deeper and deeper into that feeling and space. Imagine your breath flowing out into a vast area filled with light.

4 With each breath, let the space get larger and larger. Allow yourself to rest and be in that space in the present. If a thought appears, gently refocus on the spaciousness you have created.

5 Tell yourself that it is okay to just be. Remain in this calm space as long as you like. When ready, take a deep breath and end your session.

DISTRACTED MIND

When meditating on the breath, thoughts can pull us off track.
But distractions can originate outside ourselves in the form of
sounds, lights or smells. Labelling them helps you return to
focusing on your breath.

Benefits

- Helps you stay focused on whatever you are doing
- Increases mindfulness
- Develops patience and tolerance

If you live in a city, you are probably used to an enormous amount of sensory input – radio, TV, billboards, cars, buses, machines and smells of all kinds constantly bombard your senses. Learning to focus and calm your mind with breath meditation is a good antidote to sensory overload. Labelling external distractions when they arise during your meditation will help you develop patience and tolerance for what goes on around you. By labelling the distraction and returning to your focus on your breath, you intervene in your irritation. You learn to calm your emotions and focus your mind, regardless of what is going on around you.

Meditation

When

Try this variation on breath meditation for ten minutes, morning and evening.

Preparation

Before you begin, take extra care to make sure that your meditation space is as silent and as comfortable as possible. Notice any possible distractions and eliminate them.

Practice

1 Sit cross-legged on a cushion with your bottom slightly raised. If you can't sit cross-legged, sit on a chair. Keep your back straight, your shoulders level and relaxed and your chin parallel to the floor. Lower your eyes and focus about a metre (three feet) in front of you. Rest your hands gently on your knees.

2 Breathe normally through your nose, using your abdomen rather than your chest. Check your posture and relax any part of your body that is tense.

3 Begin counting your breath on each exhalation and when you reach ten, begin again. Notice if you are distracted by anything external such as the sound of a car starting, cooking smells from next door or changes in the light or temperature in your room. Label the distraction and return to focusing on your breath.

4 Keep track of any distractions you encounter for a week. Notice if your reaction to external distraction differs from internal thought distraction. Notice if your irritation lessens over time.

NINE-ROUND BREATHING

This is a Tibetan Buddhist breathing and purification practice, useful for balancing your mind and reducing negative thoughts before any meditation session.

Benefits

- Purifies negativity
- Calms the mind
- Prepares you for meditation

You may find it hard to settle down to meditate after work. Your mind may still be racing with thoughts left over from the day and worries about tomorrow. Nine-round breathing is a great practice to help you make the mental transition between your busy life and your meditation session. If nothing else, it will help you to calm down and relax. You will also learn to visualize and experience the Buddhist practice of purification. Nine-round breathing is a wonderful pre-meditation practice, but try it any time and anywhere to clear your mind, purify negativity and calm your soul.

Meditation

When

Practise before any meditation session or when you want to reduce negative emotions.

Preparation

Sit with your back straight. Identify any negative thoughts or emotions you would like to purify.

Practice

1 Visualize your body as completely empty and transparent. During the first round of breathing, inhale through your left nostril keeping the right closed with your left index finger. Imagine breathing in and filling your body with pure white light. While exhaling, imagine that any obsessions with sex or material possessions leave via your right nostril in the form of black smoke. Repeat three times.

2 Hold your left nostril closed with your right index finger and inhale pure white light through your right nostril. You are now clearing your anger and hatred, which leave via your left nostril in the form of black smoke. Repeat three times.

3 Breathe in white light through both nostrils. Breathe out any ignorance or mental confusion in the form of black smoke. Imagine this smoke leaving your body at the point between your eyebrows, which meditation masters refer to as your third eye or wisdom eye. Repeat three times.

4 From this calm, centred and purified state, begin your meditation practice.

DANCING FLAME

A single candle flame is a wonderful object on which to focus your mind. It draws your attention and its warmth, light and beauty are timeless and reassuring.

Benefits

- Promotes ability to focus your mind

- Calms fears

- Provides a sense of warmth and security.

Meditation

When

Try this meditation at night whenever you are feeling overwhelmed and fearful about some aspect of your life.

Preparation

If possible use an unscented, pure beeswax candle. Place your candle at eye level, away from flammable materials. Do not leave your candle unattended after your meditation.

Practice

1 Sit on a cushion or chair about a metre (three feet) away from your candle, which should be at eye level. Other lighting in the room should be low but not absent. Try to eliminate any draughts.

2 Begin your session with Nine-round breathing (see pages 58–9).

Focusing on your breath gives your mind an anchor to help calm uncontrolled thoughts. You can also focus on an external object, such as a candle flame, to achieve the same purpose.

Just as moths are drawn to a flame, so are we. Until the invention of electricity, we used candles to provide warmth, light and security during the night. We have used candles for devotion, rituals and celebrations in our churches, communities and on our home altars. They provide us with a pleasing and easy object for meditation, as well as a soothing and reassuring presence in times of fear and stress.

3 Focus on the candle flame and try to empty your mind of all thoughts. With each in-breath, allow the light and warmth of the candle flame to free your mind of any fears, anxiety or insecurity. When extraneous thoughts intervene, refocus on the candle flame in front of you.

4 Meditate in this way for ten to fifteen minutes.

FLOWING WATER

The sound of flowing water connects you with the flow of nature and reminds you that change is a natural part of life. The soothing sound blocks out harsh noises and your own mental chatter.

Benefits

- Relaxes body and mind
- Produces beneficial negative ions
- Reduces mental chatter

The peaceful sound of flowing water can calm your mind and release tension from your body. But being near flowing water can also improve your mental and physical health. In 1915, scientists discovered that when water is atomized (which happens as a result of the impact of water droplets) it produces beneficial negative ions. If you are close to flowing water, you inhale these negative ions which are absorbed into the bloodstream.

Negative ions are known to improve our well-being, and our physical and mental capacity by accelerating the delivery of oxygen to our cells. That is why you can feel so refreshed and invigorated after a spring storm or by standing next to a waterfall.

Meditation

When

Try this meditation whenever you have been cooped up for long periods in an office building or where the air is not particularly fresh or healthy.

Preparation

If you are near flowing water, meditate sitting nearby on a blanket and cushion. If you are at home, use a miniature fountain.

Practice

1 Sit on a cushion, a chair or the ground near a source of flowing water.

2 Breathe normally and focus on the sound of the water for five minutes. Try to empty your mind of all thoughts. When thoughts intervene return your focus to the sound of the flowing water.

3 With each in-breath, allow the sound of the water to deepen your relaxation in body and mind. Notice if you feel better physically when you are next to flowing water.

4 When you feel ready end your meditation. Drink a large glass of refreshing, pure water. Remind yourself to drink enough water every day.

WHERE IS MY MIND NOW?

Your mind is amazing. It can travel to the next room, to a city across the globe or into the past or the future in the blink of an eye. The problem is, sometimes your mind seems to literally have a mind of its own!

Benefits

- Demonstrates your untamed mind in action

- Helps you stay focused in the present

- Promotes physical and mental grounding

- Helps you have better control of your thoughts

You may have had the experience, while surfing the Net on a particular subject, of finding yourself at a website with no idea of how you got there. In a similar way your mind can jump seamlessly from one thought to another. You may be focused on a problem at work and in no time at all, you may find yourself thinking about something that happened at home last night. You will be hard pressed to trace how you got to what you are thinking about. This meditation exercise will help you see how your mind works, help you be more conscious of what you are thinking and help you stay grounded in the present.

Meditation

When

Practise this meditation whenever you feel your thoughts are getting too scattered and disorganized. For a more in-depth experience, practise every day for a week.

Preparation

Sit on a cushion or chair at home in a quiet setting. You can practise for a shorter period of time in any situation where you want to be grounded and in the present.

Practice

1 Breathe deeply for three breaths to make the transition from what you are doing to this meditation.

2 Begin counting your breaths and when thoughts intervene, note the time and location of your thoughts. For instance, if you are thinking of your childhood in your home town, note 'in my past, home town' and return to focus on your breath.

3 Meditate in this way for ten minutes. When you stop, write down all the physical locations of your thoughts and whether they took place in the past or the future. Keep a daily log and note where your mind has travelled. In between meditation sessions, try to be conscious of your thoughts and stay focused in the present.

SACRED WORDS

Reciting a mantra or sacred Sanskrit words can help you focus, pacify and transform your mind. Mantra recitation is an aspect of Buddhist/Hindu spirituality, but you can use mantra recitation for mental and physical relaxation.

Benefits

- Relaxes your body
- Calms your mind
- Develops compassion

Meditation

When

Practise mantra recitation when and where you like.

Preparation

If possible use Buddhist prayer beads with 108 beads or use a popular prayer bead bracelet. These are easily ordered from suppliers on the Internet. If you don't have any prayer beads, simply count on your fingers.

One of the most famous Tibetan Buddhist mantras is 'OM MANI PADME HUM'. Known simply as the MANI, it is the mantra of the supremely compassionate Avalokiteshvara, the Tibetan Buddhist embodiment of compassion.

One popular way of employing the MANI is to think compassionately towards all beings in the universe while slowly repeating the mantra at least 21 and preferably 108 times. Include human beings, animals, fish, birds and insects. Remember to include yourself as an object of your compassion. Although it is not necessary, mantra recitation is often practised using prayer beads or a Buddhist rosary called a *mala*. In Tibet, mantras are considered very powerful. In addition to being recited, sacred words or mantras are printed on prayer flags. The mantras or prayers are carried on the wind and in turn bless the environment and its beings.

Practice

1 Sit cross-legged on a cushion in a quiet, private space, where you won't disturb anyone.

2 Breathe deeply for a minute or so to clear your mind. Then begin reciting the mantra OM MANI PADME HUM slowly in a low, quiet voice. When thoughts intervene return to focusing on the mantra.

3 After a few minutes, continue to say the mantra and begin visualizing your words reaching all living beings and relieving them of their suffering. Be sure to include yourself. Do this for 108 recitations or one round of a traditional Buddhist rosary or *mala*.

4 End your meditation by sitting quietly and focusing on your breath for two minutes.

GREGORIAN CHANT

You will find Gregorian or plain chant, the Church music of the early Middle Ages, reassuring and calming. Lending an ear to this ancient plainsong no longer involves devotion, but when listening, keep in mind that these are the sounds of mortals presuming to address their God.

Benefits

- Lowers blood pressure and heart rate
- Steadies pulse and breathing
- Quiets the mind
- Uplifts and renews the spirit

In this busy, fast-paced age your mind may wander in search for something more meaningful and comforting. You may feel you need something more soothing for your body and soul. Research conducted in France in the1960s by Dr Alfred Tomitas found that listening to Gregorian chant heals the body and calms the spirit. In addition to mending spiritual illness, it may provide relief from hypertension, migraine headaches, ulcers and heart attacks. He found listening to chant slows the metabolism, steadies the pulse and breathing, and quiets the mind.

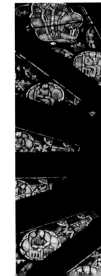

According to his theory, there are two kinds of sound: discharge sounds – those that tire, fatigue and drain the listener; and charge sounds – those that give energy and health. According to Dr Tomitas, Gregorian chant may be the most potent charge sound to promote strength and vitality.

Meditation

When

Listen to Gregorian chant anywhere and at any time, but especially when you are experiencing stress.

Preparation

Buy a CD of Gregorian chant at your local music store or borrow one from your library. You can also find radio stations that 'stream' Gregorian chant on the Web.

Practice

1 Play Gregorian chant in your car, on a portable music player, or on your home stereo or computer.

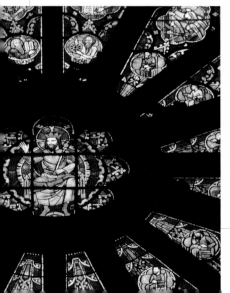

2 Breathe deeply a few times. Empty your mind of thought and worry and let the sound of the chant wash over you. Mentally join those who are offering praise to God, Buddha or your Higher Power.

3 Listen as long as you like. Notice afterwards if you feel calmer and less stressed. If you meditate on Gregorian chant regularly, notice if your health and mental state improve.

HIMALAYAN SINGING BOWL

Himalayan singing bowls are bells that look like a bowls and are played with a mallet. Cultures that use singing bowls for meditation include Tibet, Nepal, Mongolia, Sikkim, China, India and Bhutan.

Benefits

- Heals through sympathetic vibration
- Grounds your body and emotions
- Induces alpha brain waves
- Relaxes your body and mind

Many cultures and religions revere sound so deeply that they believe sound called the universe into being. Every atom, molecule, cell, gland and organ of your body absorbs and emits sound, vibrating at a frequency of about 8 cycles per second, the basic frequency of the electromagnetic field of the Earth. Scientific studies show that sound can produce changes in your autonomic, immune and endocrine systems. Dr Mitchell Gaynor at Strang-Cornell Cancer Prevention Center in the US is using singing bowls in his medical practice with cancer patients. You will find playing singing bowls a wonderful addition to your meditation practice.

Meditation

When

Try practising singing bowl meditation
alone in a quiet place at the same time
every day.

Preparation

Buy or borrow a Himalayan or Tibetan
singing bowl.

Practice

1 Sit on a cushion or a comfortable
chair with your singing bowl. Hold the
bowl in your hands for a while. Notice its
weight, shape and texture.

2 If you have a larger bowl, hold it in
the palm of your hand. If you have a
smaller one, hold it balanced on your
fingertips. Be sure not to touch the side
as this will dampen the sound. You can
also just rest the bowl on a padded
cushion next to you.

3 Strike the bowl with a padded
mallet. Listen to the sound and feel
the vibration. Let it ring out and fade.
Imagine that your suffering and that of all
other beings fades away with the sound.

4 Instead of striking the bowl you can
'sing' the bowl. Hold a wooden
mallet against the rim and very slowly rub
it around the bowl applying even
pressure. The vibration will gradually
build to a strong tone and will sing at its
fullest. Imagine you are healing any
illness you may have as your body tunes
itself to the bowl's vibrations.

STAR-GAZING

There is nothing more beautiful and inspiring than a clear, star-filled night sky. Take time to bask in its beauty and meditate on the vastness of the universe and your place in it.

Benefits

- Provides perspective on your problems

- Helps you to experience the vastness of the universe

- Relaxes your body and mind

Meditation

When

Choose a clear night when the weather is comfortable for you to be outside.

Preparation

Find a comfortable blanket or a folding *chaise lounge* that allows you to be more or less prone. Take a torch and head for as dark an area as you can find, preferably in the country, away from street and city lights. Bring a jacket in case you get cold.

Your busy life may keep you on a treadmill – running from work to home and back again. It is important to take a break and experience the awesome beauty of the night sky. Looking up, you will no doubt feel dwarfed by the magnificence and size of the universe. Faced with such an inconceivable vastness, your unpaid gas bill will not matter as much, your anxiety over work will fade and your body and mind will find much-needed relief from the push of everyday life.

Next time the world seems to be too much for you, wait for the evening then look up at the sky. There is nothing that the world can do to compete. Submit to the moment and feel a part of the cosmos, and everything and everyone in it.

Practice

1 Stretch out under the stars. Breathe deeply for a few minutes and get comfortable.

2 Allow yourself to 'fall into' the night sky above you. Let whatever thoughts or emotions that emerge, enter your awareness and gently move on. Stay as long as you like.

3 When you return home, write a few paragraphs about your experience and any realizations you had about your problems and how to deal with them.

EMOTIONAL MIND

When meditating on the breath, emotions as much as thoughts and external distractions can pull you off track. Labelling them helps shed light on your emotional patterns.

Benefits

- Reveals which emotions dominate your mind

- Helps you extract yourself from negative emotions

- Promotes the ability to focus and concentrate in moments of emotional stress

Emotions such as joy, sadness, jealousy, anger, resentment, pride and depression are triggered by external realities and also by your thoughts. There is nothing wrong with having emotions, but problems occur if you allow them to take over your life. By recognizing and identifying emotions as they arise during meditation, you may learn how your thoughts can spiral you into an agitated emotional state.

For example, while meditating on your breath, you may think of a relative, and then think of an occasion when he hurt you. You are then engulfed in a rage over his behaviour, your heart beats faster, your face flushes and you forget you were trying to meditate. In this case you are being held hostage by your emotions. Becoming aware of how your thoughts generate your emotions will help you understand where you are stuck emotionally.

Meditation

When

Try this variation on breath meditation for ten minutes, morning and evening.

Preparation

Take extra care to ensure that your meditation space is as silent and as comfortable as possible. Review any emotions you are aware of as you sit down to meditate.

Practice

1 Sit cross-legged on a cushion with your bottom slightly raised. If you can't sit cross-legged, sit on a chair. Keep your back straight, your shoulders level and relaxed and your chin parallel to the floor. Lower your eyes and focus about a metre (three feet) in front of you. Rest your hands gently on your knees.

2 Breathe normally through your nose, using your abdomen rather than your chest. Check your posture and relax any part of your body that is tense.

3 Begin counting your breath on each exhalation and when you reach ten, begin again. Notice what emotion arises when a thought occurs. Label the emotion, such as 'happiness' or 'fear' and return to your focus on your breath.

4 As you meditate, accept any emotion that arises. Begin to notice how emotions can be as ephemeral as your thoughts.

5 Meditate in this way for one week. Notice if you become more aware of your emotions in your day-to-day life. See if it becomes easier to accept your emotions and perhaps not be as 'carried away' by them.

MOTHER EARTH

We spend a lot of time in cars, indoors and on paved streets and sidewalks. It is always good, from time to time, to physically reconnect with our Mother.

Benefits

- Reconnects you physically with the Earth
- Grounds your thinking and emotions
- Simultaneously stimulates and relaxes your body and mind

The Earth, literally the dirt and grass beneath your feet, holds and nurtures you like a mother. You survive because she supplies your food and water. Physically reconnecting with Mother Earth helps strengthen your body and relax your mind. She encourages you to recognize your connectedness with the rest of the universe. Standing barefoot on her 'body' can be very healing in times of high stress and alienation. The delicious feel of the resilient ground and soft green grass poking through your toes stimulates you from head to toe. At the same time, you will feel a deep relaxation as your tension drains away.

Meditation

When

Practise this meditation outdoors in pleasant weather during the daytime whenever you are feeling especially disconnected, lonely or unloved.

Preparation

Locate a secluded grassy area away from traffic and other noise.

Practice

1 Enter your secluded grassy area barefoot. Find a level area where you can stand away from overhanging trees. Stand with your feet shoulder-width apart and let your arms hang loosely at your sides. Breathe gently and deeply for a few minutes.

2 Visualize a strong energy flowing up and down your spine, and then down through both legs. Stay with this powerful energy as it moves up and down your spine and legs. Now imagine that this energy lengthens and extends through your feet deeply into the ground and for miles into the Earth.

3 Now imagine the nurturing energy of Mother Earth returning through your feet and up your legs and spine. Feel the energy as it flows through you, relaxing and rejuvenating your body and mind.

4 Enjoy this energy exchange for as long as you like. When you feel ready, stretch out on the grass, with arms and legs apart and rest.

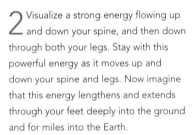

77

GREET YOUR DAY

Your daily ritual may involve getting up to an alarm, rushing to shower, dress and eat and then dashing to work. For a change, set your alarm early and begin your day with the sunrise, Mother Nature's daily expression of hope and celebration of new beginnings.

Benefits

- Helps you let go of the past and begin anew
- Encourages hope
- Calms and centres you for the day ahead

Meditation

When

Do this meditation outdoors at sunrise.

Preparation

Gather your chair or cushion, and perhaps a blanket to protect you from the dew on the grass from the night before. Dress warmly.

You may already be setting your alarm early enough to see the sunrise, but chances are you are busy getting ready for work. If so, try this meditation on the weekend. Set your alarm for a little before sunrise, when the night sky is beginning to lighten and the birds are beginning to sing.

Most contemplative monks and nuns, Catholic and Buddhist, begin their day around around 3 or 4 am. They greet the first light with prayer and meditation. Native Americans of the Lakota tribe greet the sun rising as the manifestation of *Wakan Tanka*, the equivalent of God in the Judeo-Christian tradition. Greeting the dawn is a wonderful way to begin your day – in sync with the rhythms of nature and in touch with your spirit.

Practice

1 Find a spot facing east and take your seat just before sunrise. Take a few deep breaths and settle into a comfortable position.

2 Bring your attention to the sounds of the birds and animals stirring, the Earth below you and the sky above. Feel your own energy and be conscious that you are the meeting place where Earth meets sky.

3 As the sky lightens in the east and the night gives way to day, let go of any sense of failure or regret. Greet the morning with tenderness and feel tenderness towards yourself and others. Acknowledge there has been loss and celebrate a new beginning.

4 Sit in quiet contemplation until you are ready to start the day.

TIBETAN SUNSET

Use this meditation when you are depressed and despondent about your life. Let a beautiful sunset lift you out of the doldrums.

Benefits

- Helps with depression

- Facilitates letting go of pain and disappointment

- Calms agitation and worry

Meditation

When

Practise this meditation at the end of the day, whenever you feel overwhelmed and depressed.

Preparation

Find a good place to view the sunset on a clear day.

Practice

1 Stand facing west towards the setting sun. Let yourself feel your depression and your worries fully. Contemplate the fact that everything is impermanent, even the terrible mistakes you may have made or your ongoing depression that you can't seem to heal.

2 As the sun begins to go down over the horizon, lift yourself up on to your toes. As it sinks further visualize all your worries, problems, failures and mistakes going with it. Stand on your toes until the sun disappears completely.

Sometimes you just have a bad day, a very bad day. You may even have a string of them and feel overwhelmed and depressed by your perceived failures and mistakes. Give yourself a lift, literally, with this unique meditation which is practised in old Tibet. Buddhists use this meditation to help let go of the negativities of the day and meditate on the truth that all things are impermanent, both positive and negative. This meditation gives you a lift because you literally stand on your toes.

3 Lower yourself back to your normal stance. Imagine that all your problems disappeared with the setting sun. Now focus on the present and the future. Visualize yourself as starting with a clean slate, with renewed energy and positive regard for yourself and all others.

FLOWER POWER

Flowers are exquisitely beautiful and a potent source of inspiration. Meditating on flowers elevates your spirits and soothes your soul.

Benefits

- Provides a calming influence in times of stress
- Inspires appreciation of nature's beauty
- Encourages healing when ill
- Provides comfort in times of sorrow

A single rose, an iris, a lily – all bring to mind a fantastic, almost shocking beauty. They focus our attention and both energize and calm our stressed-out bodies and minds. Besides being overwhelmingly beautiful, they are rich with meaning and symbolism. For Christians, the daffodil symbolizes the resurrection of Christ and violets, the Virgin Mary. The prophet Mohammed saw violets as symbols of his teachings. They are also connected to Persephone and the hereafter – she was strolling through a field of violets when Hades kidnapped her.

Meditation

When

Meditate on flowers when you are struggling with an illness or with the loss of a loved one.

Preparation

Pick a flower from your garden or purchase one at a shop. Place your single flower in a vase on a table in front of you, just below eye level.

Practice

1 Sit in a chair or on a cushion. Take a few deep breaths and set aside any worries or distractions. Focus on the flower in front of you. Empty your mind of all thoughts and breathe normally.

2 Notice the flower's unique beauty. Breathe in its scent. Visualize the perfume filling your body and healing any illness or health problem you may be experiencing. If you are grieving for a loved one, let your tears flow and allow your flower's essence to soothe your broken heart.

3 End your meditation when your emotions are calm and your breathing is deep and normal.

Clearly, flowers have had a powerful influence on humans, and for good reason. Their fragile beauty captivates our imagination and their very presence uplifts and heals. If you haven't paid that much attention to flowers, get to know them as objects of meditation.

CENTRING PRAYER

Most religious traditions practise some form of centring prayer. This centring prayer meditation is based on the Christian tradition.

Benefits

- Connects you with the sacred
- Centres you in your spiritual practice
- Counteracts societal focus on materialism
- Balances emotions

Meditation

When

Practise centring prayer meditation whenever you feel disconnected from your spiritual life.

Preparation

Go to a bookshop or library and explore books on spirituality that appeal to you.

This prayer is drawn from ancient prayer practices of the Christian contemplative tradition, notably *The Cloud of Unknowing*, written by fourteenth-century monk St John of the Cross and St Teresa of Avila. It was distilled into this simple method of prayer in the 1970s by three Trappist monks, William Meninger, Basil Pennington and Thomas Keating.

Centring prayer is based on meditation on a single word that you consider sacred. The intention is to invite God or the Sacred into your heart and your life, to provide balance and guidance in a very secular world.

Practice

1 Start with a spiritual text that inspires you. Allow a word to emerge from your reading that resonates within you; for example, God, Buddha, Jesus, love or peace. This sacred word expresses your intent for God or the Sacred to enter your heart and be present in your life.

2 Sit comfortably with your eyes closed and introduce your word inwardly.

When you become aware of thoughts or distractions, bring yourself back to your sacred word. Meditate in this way for 20 minutes.

3 At the end of your prayer remain silent with your eyes closed for a few more minutes. Notice the effects of centring prayer on your daily life.

PEACE ON EARTH

Strife and conflict dominate world headlines. Practise this meditation if you feel overwhelmed and saddened by the current state of world affairs.

Benefits

- Lessens fear and anxiety
- Promotes personal and world peace
- Empowers when feeling powerless

Television and the Internet provide you with 24-hour, instantaneous news. Often that news is about violence, war and conflict of all kinds. It is easy to feel overwhelmed, hopeless and powerless, or to bury your feelings only to have them manifest in sleepless nights or other stress-related problems. Try this meditation when you are aware that conflicts are causing you stress, whether in your personal life or half-way around the world.

Meditation

When

Practise this meditation when you are feeling afraid, overwhelmed and hopeless about the state of the world.

Preparation

Read the newspaper or listen to the news for a few days. Identify any fears or anxieties that come up as a result of what you read or hear.

Practice

1 Find a quiet place at home or outdoors. Sit in any way you find comfortable. Breathe deeply for a few minutes.

2 Think about a particular conflict that affects you. Try not to take sides, favouring one warring group over another. Acknowledge that both the aggressor and those transgressed upon are suffering.

3 Generate the desire for all beings involved to heal their anger and pain. Include yourself in this wish. Visualize a sacred being, God, Buddha, Krishna, the Virgin Mary or your higher power. Imagine a cooling and healing white light emanating from that being to you, filling your body and calming any anger or fear you may feel.

4 From your heart, send out light to those at war. Visualize that they have ended their conflict and are beginning to live in peace. End your meditation session when you feel ready.

EMOTIONAL STORM

Once in a while, you may find yourself in rough emotional weather. You may even feel that you have been hijacked by your anger or jealousy. Use this meditation to calm the storm.

Benefits

- Calms anger and other negative emotions

- Heals and transforms negative emotions

- Promotes compassion for yourself and others

If you are feeling consumed by anger or rage about a family member or a situation at work, meditation is a great way to calm down and get some perspective on the situation and your emotions. Chances are that if you are feeling angry, underneath you may be feeling hurt, defensive or confused. The antidote to your anger is patience and compassion with yourself and the person with whom you are angry. Invoking a higher being who is the embodiment of compassion will cool the hot fires of your emotions and give you a little space to assess the situation in a more balanced and caring way.

Meditation

When

Try this whenever you are caught in the throes of anger or jealousy.

Preparation

Find a quiet place away from the person or situation that provoked your anger, where you will not be disturbed for at least 15 minutes.

Practice

1 Sit comfortably with your spine straight. If you are feeling too bad to sit up, lie down flat on your back. Calm yourself by taking a few deep breaths, then breathe naturally.

2 Now focus your attention on the emotions you are feeling. Try not to analyze them. Instead, concentrate on just feeling them.

3 Imagine the face of the most loving, caring, compassionate being you can think of. It could be God, Buddha, the Virgin Mary, a special teacher or any other being. It could be a being you don't know. You may think of it as a manifestation of Spirit or as just a caring and compassionate being.

4 Spend a few minutes in the presence of this being. Talk to them out loud or silently about your anger, rage or jealousy.

5 Offer your negative emotions up to this loving being to be healed and transformed. Sit quietly for a few minutes and end your meditation.

LIVING MINDFULLY

MEDITATIONS FOR LIVING MINDFULLY

Now that you have calmed and stabilized your mind, you are ready to explore meditations that help you be more mindful and aware. By practising mindfulness meditation, you learn to focus your awareness and expand your consciousness.

You can practise mindfulness anywhere or any time but by sitting in meditation you enhance your ability to bring mindfulness into your daily life. At work you will be better able to stay present in meetings, complete projects and eliminate distractions. Your relationships will improve when you are capable of being one hundred per cent present to your loved one.

Living mindfully in the present moment greatly enriches your experience of living. You will begin to appreciate the power and beauty all around you – from the astonishing colour of a deep red rose, to the sensitive face of an old woman on the train. Your world will expand and deepen.

Mindfulness is not only directed outwardly. Through focused meditations, you will explore your vast internal landscape and expand your understanding of your mind, your body and your emotions. You will begin to see your mental and emotional habits and patterns and decide whether they help you or not.

The first meditation, 'Glass half-full', will help you appreciate what you may be taking for granted, while 'Monkey mind' and 'What are you thinking?' will help you to be mindful of your thoughts. 'You have a body' reconnects you with your body and 'Do I have an attitude?' helps you be aware of three basic attitudes that you have towards anything and anyone. If you want to work on having awareness without bias or judgement, try 'Autumn leaf'. Try 'Conscious listening' for learning how to listen with full attention. 'A tasteful meditation' and 'Ripe fruit' teach sensual awareness. If you want to experience subtle body sensations, try 'In a heartbeat'.

'Emotional mindfulness' needs no explanation, while 'Do the dishes' and 'Shopping' will forever change your experience of these activities. If you are feeling confused about spending, 'Compassionate consumption' helps you buy mindfully. 'Only now' brings home that point. Give up the stress of multi-tasking with 'One thing at a time'. 'The eyes have it' teaches mindfulness with a partner, while 'Media monitor' and 'Space cadet' are for the escapist in you. And last and perhaps most important, 'Life is short' gives you motivation to be mindful of every precious minute.

GLASS HALF-FULL

It is easy to take what you have for granted and be chronically dissatisfied. Focusing on what blessings you have can transform your mind and your life.

Benefits

- Provides antidote to chronic dissatisfaction
- Increases your awareness of your blessings
- Helps you stay in the present moment

It is so easy to be caught up in feeling a chronic sense of lack, encouraged by a culture that says you never have enough and are never good enough. You may find yourself fixated on that new car, a better relationship, new towels or a different place to live as the key to making you a happier person. But you may have noticed, seeing your glass half-empty all the time makes for a miserable life. Always looking to the future means you aren't really present in the life you have right now. By meditating on gratitude on a daily basis, you will reduce your dissatisfaction and increase your contentment with the life you have. Happiness, you will discover, is ultimately a state of mind.

Meditation

When

If you are preoccupied with
wanting things you don't have.

Preparation

Write down everything you want that you don't have.
Then write down ten things you are grateful for.

Practice

1 Find time to be alone in a place
where you will not be disturbed. Sit
in any way that makes you comfortable.
After doing the preliminary exercise
above, read over the ten things that you
have listed.

2 Generate a sincere sense of
gratitude for each item on your list.
If you are grateful for your health, feel
thankful for your good fortune. If you
have a car, no matter what condition, be
sincerely grateful to have transportation.
If you have a partner, think of their
wonderful qualities and be grateful that
they are a part of your life.

3 After you have gone through your
list, sit quietly and thank yourself,
God, the universe, or whomever or
whatever you choose, for the gifts you
have been given. Resolve, on a daily
basis, to be mindful and grateful for the
blessings you have.

MONKEY MIND

While you are awake, you are thinking constantly. Your mind may jump from one thought to another, like a monkey leaping from branch to branch. This meditation helps you to be more mindful of what you are thinking.

Benefits

- Teaches you to be mindful of your thoughts
- Reveals the often erratic nature of your thinking process
- Helps you to focus and concentrate

You may have had the experience of driving off to the shops or work, then getting lost in thought and 'waking up' as you pull into the parking lot. During the drive you had hundreds of thoughts, images and impressions cross your mind. Some of those thoughts triggered emotions, which in turn led to other thoughts. It is as if the car was on automatic and drove itself.

This meditation is designed to help you observe your mind and its tendency to jump continuously from one thought to another. It will help you be more mindful of what you are thinking, which in turn will help you bring your focus and concentration to whatever subject or task you choose.

Meditation

When

This meditation helps when you are chronically distracted, feeling scattered in your thinking or having difficulty concentrating.

Preparation

Before practising this meditation, try watching your mind for a few days as you drive your car or ride on public transport. Begin to notice how one thought jumps to another. Have ready a pencil, paper and a watch. This meditation can be practised anywhere, anytime. If you want to sit formally on your own in meditation posture, that is fine too.

Practice

1 Take a few deep breaths to signal that you are going to focus on this meditation. Immediately begin to watch your thoughts. Notice how quickly and seamlessly your mind jumps from one idea, impression and thought to another.

2 Think back to a few minutes ago and try to remember what you were thinking. Trace how you got to what you are thinking now.

3 Look at a watch or a clock for 60 seconds. Make hash marks with a pencil every time your thoughts change during the minute.

4 Bring this new awareness of 'monkey mind' into your daily life. Try to be more mindful of what you are thinking, rather than getting lost in thought.

WHAT ARE YOU THINKING?

Noting the content of your thoughts when you meditate on your breath will help you to discover patterns in your thinking and be more mindful of your thought processes.

Benefits

- Helps you be mindful of your thinking patterns
- Provides insight on worries and concerns
- Helps identify and change negative thought patterns

You can learn a great deal about yourself by being mindful of your thoughts as they arise during breath meditation. You can identify where you might be 'stuck' emotionally and intellectually. Over time you will notice certain 'ruts' in your thinking, such as worries over whether your partner really loves you or not, or anger about your boss's attitude towards you. By labelling the content of recurring thoughts, you will gain a better perspective on your thinking. As a consequence, you will be able to change negative or unhealthy patterns, such as being judgmental or overly fearful.

Meditation

When

Try this variation on breath meditation for ten minutes, morning and evening.

Preparation

Find a quiet place at home where you will be undisturbed. Before you begin, ask yourself if there is any pattern to your thinking, or do you have recurring thoughts. Do you worry about money or fantasize frequently about an ideal sexual partner? Do you spend time figuring out how to get revenge for past hurts?

Practice

1 Sit cross-legged on a cushion with your bottom slightly raised. If you can't sit cross-legged, sit on a chair. Keep your back straight, your shoulders level and relaxed and your chin parallel to the floor. Lower your eyes and focus about a metre (three feet) in front of you. Rest your hands gently on your knees.

2 Breathe normally through your nose, using your abdomen rather than your chest. Check your posture and relax any part of your body that is tense.

3 Begin counting your breath and when you reach ten, begin again. When thoughts intervene, note the content. For instance, if you thought about money problems, silently note 'worrying about money' and return to counting your breath.

4 Meditate for about ten minutes. At the end of your session write down which thoughts emerged. Do this for one week and notice any recurring patterns. Notice if your thinking about something or someone changes.

YOU HAVE A BODY

Meditating on mindfulness of physical sensations allows you to become more aware of your body. If you have been split off mentally from your body, this meditation will help you reconnect.

Benefits

- Helps you become more aware of your body
- Promotes balance of body and mind
- Reveals connection between physical and psychological symptoms

Are you one of those people who is conscious only from the neck up? Are you unaware of how your body feels most of the time? Reconnecting with your body by becoming mindful of bodily sensations, such as muscular tension, the feel of clothing next to your skin or a stiff neck, will help you understand your emotions better and create the conditions for enhanced physical health. You may not be aware that you clench your jaw when you are angry or that you barely breathe when you are afraid. Maybe you hunch over most of the time and don't even know it. Becoming aware of your body sensations, over time, will help you stay healthier, mentally and physically.

Meditation

When

Try this mindfulness meditation whenever you feel disconnected from your body.

Preparation

Before meditating, stretch out on your bed or the floor. Scan your entire body beginning at your toes to the crown of your head and notice any physical sensations or areas of tension.

Practice

1 Sit on a cushion or a chair keeping your back straight as possible, yet relaxed. Calm your mind by observing your breath.

2 Shift the focus on your breath to another part of your body. Choose a spot that is easy to feel, like your neck or your knee. Focus all your awareness on that spot. Try to merge with any sensations you may feel. Observe the sensation without judging it as pleasant or unpleasant.

3 Is the sensation a tightness, a burning or a tingling? Is it a combination of many sensations? Do they change over time? Keep your awareness on the spot. If thoughts intrude, return your focus to the spot.

4 If you want, switch to another part of your body and repeat the same exercise. When ready, end your meditation. Try to bring this mindfulness of your body into your daily life.

)O I HAVE AN ATTITUDE?

Your attitude towards anyone or anything you encounter is usually one of either attraction, aversion or indifference. Using meditation to become aware of your attitudes leads you to greater mental balance and stability.

Benefits

- Promotes peace and equanimity

- Helps you deal with life's ups and downs

- Reminds that everything changes over time

Our habit of sorting everything into three judgemental categories is ultimately exhausting and painful. Clinging to our attitudes belies the truth that all things change. Cultivating a sense of openness and acceptance will help us weather life's difficulties with grace and flexibility.

Meditation

When

Try this meditation when you are feeling particularly judgemental or self-centred in your dealings with others.

Preparation

A few days before this meditation, begin to notice how you organize experiences and people you encounter into one of three categories: like, dislike or neutral.

Practice

1 Find a quiet place indoors where you can be alone. Sit on a cushion or on a straight-backed chair. Chose one object, a situation or a person on which to focus for this meditation session. Mentally take time to create a vivid and detailed image of your chosen object.

2 As you meditate, allow your feelings to arise and carefully note your attitude. Don't suppress a negative attitude or edit it to what you think you should feel. Accept without judgement any attitude you may have.

3 Ask yourself a series of questions to explore your attitude more closely. Have you always felt this way towards this object or person? What led to you feeling this way? What could cause your attitude to change? Note any bodily sensations that arise.

4 As you deepen your understanding of you attitude, remind yourself that what you feel is only what you feel today. Try to cultivate an attitude of equanimity; that is, not feeling any judgement at all. Remind yourself that attitudes, like everything else, change over time.

AUTUMN LEAF

To perceive without bias or judgement is a difficult task for anyone. Unfortunately, labelling and judgements prevent you from experiencing life directly. This simple awareness meditation will help you to experience nature more deeply and joyfully.

Benefits

- Deepens experience of nature
- Enhances sensual experience
- Promotes relaxation and sense of connectedness to all life

In the twenty-first century, your experience of nature may come primarily from television and books rather than from being outdoors yourself. These interpretations of nature invite categorizing and judging: the most beautiful holiday spot, the most rare flower or award-winning tomatoes. Instead of intellectualizing nature, return to her in person whenever you have a chance and experience her directly.

Meditation

When

Practise this meditation when you feel separated from nature and distanced from your own direct experience of life.

Preparation

Choose a park or woods in which to walk, preferably in autumn when all the leaves are turning.

Practice

1 Walk for a few minutes in the park or woods while focusing on your breath. Try to empty your mind of all thoughts.

2 Stop walking, pick up a fallen leaf and hold it in your hand. Notice if you are judging the leaf in any way – for its appearance, size or colour, or if you are comparing it to another you didn't pick up. Try to let go of any thoughts or judgements about the leaf.

3 Begin by simply taking in the leaf visually as if you were a Martian and had never seen one before. Notice its exquisite shape, colour and the tiny delicate veins spreading from its centre. If it has blemishes from insects or decay, see them as equally beautiful and perfect.

4 Spend time being with the leaf in this way. Try to bring this way of experiencing the leaf to the rest of your life. Notice if you feel more relaxed, more fulfilled and more aware of the beauty all around you.

ƆNSCIOUS LISTENING

In New York, it is said that there is only talking and waiting to talk. It is meant to be funny, but it is probably more true than not. This meditation helps you learn to listen to others with your full attention.

Benefits

- Teaches you to listen mindfully

- Promotes empathy

- Reduces self-centredness

Meditation

When

Try this when communication with others is not going well.

Preparation

Choose a person with whom you would like to have better communication. Before you meet with them, visualize them in your mind's eye. Contemplate that they are just like you – they want to be happy and want to avoid suffering.

Practice

1 When you meet with your chosen person, make sure only you and the other person are having a conversation. Ask them a question.

2 When he or she responds, make an effort to not anticipate what will be said or begin thinking about what you will say in response. Try to listen deeply to what the person is saying – with their voice, emotions

Not all meditations have to take place while sitting on a cushion away from other people. You can learn to meditate or direct your attention and awareness in any situation: at the office, with family members or even with the clerk at your bank.

and body language. Work on not judging or projecting yourself or your ideas on to what he or she is communicating.

3 Notice how much more you hear when you give another person this kind of focused sympathetic attention. See if this improves the quality of your relationships.

A TASTEFUL MEDITATION

We not only have fast food, we have fast eating! Try slowing down to experience mindfully and taste your food.

Benefits

- Promotes mindful, conscious eating
- Helps you to switch to healthy foods
- Increases sensitivity to taste

Eating slowly and mindfully increases the pleasure of eating. You will not only taste more, but by eating consciously, you will be more likely to eat healthier foods.

Meditation

When

You can do this meditation at home, whenever you have a meal.

Preparation

Prepare a healthy, balanced meal.

Practice

1 Arrange everything on the your table and sit down. Do not start eating immediately; take time to relax and settle your mind. Set your intention to eat with mindfulness in order to be a healthier person. Express gratitude for the food you are about to eat.

2 Pick up your fork and place a bite of food in your mouth. Put your fork back on to the table. Chew carefully and thoroughly. Focus on the sensations on your tongue, teeth and throat as you swallow. Notice the taste. Is it sweet, salty, sour, bitter, or flavoured with spices and herbs? Most likely you will notice a combination.

3 When you have completely experienced the taste sensations from the first bite, pick up your fork and take another. Watch what arises in your mind. Are you frustrated with eating so slowly? Are you anticipating the next bite before you finish the one you have? Are you eating after your stomach is full?

4 Try to let go of all your emotional baggage about eating and simply savour the tastes of the food, as if you were eating for the first time. Try to bring mindfulness to your everyday eating.

RIPE FRUIT

The Slow Food movement, which started in Italy advocates restoring sensuous pleasure and quality ingredients to cooking and dining. This meditation will help you be more mindful of your senses.

Benefits

- Promotes mindfulness of the senses

- Helps you eat more mindfully

- Increases pleasure

Meditation

When

Practise when you have been eating poorly for a period of time or feel a lack of joy and pleasure in your life.

Preparation

Go to a farmers' market, if possible, and select a ripe, organically grown piece of fruit. It could be a plum, an apple, a pear or a beautiful strawberry. Choose whatever makes your mouth water in anticipation.

Practice

1 Place your piece of fruit on a beautiful plate on your dining table. Take a seat at your table.

2 Spend a little time looking at the fruit. Notice its colour, shape and texture. If it is a plum, look at its beautiful purple skin. If it is a strawberry, notice the tiny seeds on its surface. Pick it up and examine it carefully. Put it to your nose and inhale its heady fragrance.

A piece of ripe, organic fruit, unspoiled by chemicals, waxes or sprays, is a delight to the nose, the eye and the tongue. Eating it slowly and mindfully will increase your pleasure and serve as reminder to pay more attention to your senses in all areas of your life.

3 Now close your eyes and slowly take your first bite. Let the taste of the fruit explode in your mouth. Chew it very slowly, savouring the flesh and juices. Continue eating the fruit in this manner.

4 When you have eaten the entire fruit, notice any aftertaste. Sit quietly and express gratitude for such a lovely, sensuous experience.

IN A HEARTBEAT

Meditating on subtle body sensations, such as your heartbeat, increases your mindfulness of your body during everyday activities. Becoming mindful of your body and your surroundings helps you stay rooted in the present.

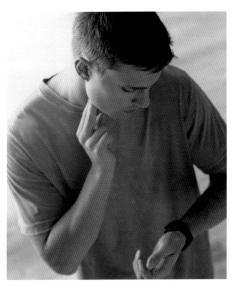

Benefits

- Deepens your mindfulness of body sensations

- Helps you appreciate your body and your life

- Encourages living in the present moment

Your heart is magnificent. It keeps you alive day after day, pumping away, not asking anything of you except that you eat well and exercise once in a while. Paying attention to your beautiful heartbeat may inspire you to take better care of yourself.

Meditation

When

Meditate on your heartbeat once a week, when you have at least 20 minutes of uninterrupted time.

Preparation

Practise the meditation 'You have a body' on pages 100–101 sometime before trying this meditation.

Practice

1 Sit on a cushion or a straight-backed chair in a quiet place where you will be undisturbed by noise or other intrusions. Focus on your breath for a few minutes.

2 Pick a spot on your body where you can feel your heartbeat. It may be your chest, your neck, your wrist or another place where you can feel your blood pumping. Focus on this spot for a few minutes.

3 Extend your awareness to all your veins and arteries, and feel the blood circulating through your heart to the rest of your body. Notice if your heart speeds up or slows down. If thoughts intervene, bring your awareness and focus back to your heartbeat.

4 End your meditation when you are ready. Then express gratitude for having such a marvellous body and a wonderful heart that serves you so faithfully day in and day out. Resolve to take care of your physical body as best you can.

EMOTIONAL MINDFULNESS

You were introduced to your emotions in the last section on calming and centring when you learned to label your emotions and return to your breath. In this meditation you actually meditate on your emotional state.

Benefits

- Helps you recognize that emotional states are transitory
- Increases acceptance of your emotions
- Helps you to not identify with your emotions

Some familiar emotional states are joy, sadness, jealousy, anger, resentment, excitement, pride and depression. You may experience any of the above as a result of life experiences. Sometimes they arise from your attitudes; for example, if you are attached to someone you may get jealous if they pay attention to others. If you judge someone negatively you may feel anger towards them. Your emotions are not a problem. We are all emotional creatures. The problem comes when you identify with your anger. Instead of saying to yourself, 'I am angry' try saying 'there is anger'. This helps keep your emotions from blowing up and taking over. Being mindful of your emotions will help you accept them and also stay in control of them.

Meditation

When

Practise emotional mindfulness meditation for 20 minutes whenever you feel emotionally overwhelmed or out of control.

Preparation

Practise the 'Emotional mind' meditation on pages 74–5 sometime before trying this one.

Practice

1 Sit comfortably on a cushion or chair. Bring your awareness to whatever emotion or emotions you are feeling in this moment. Are you happy, sad, depressed, angry, confused or fearful?

2 Examine your dominant emotional state as an observer, trying not to identify with the emotion. If it is unpleasant, stay with it. If you feel you shouldn't have this emotion, don't repress it. Be accepting and nonjudgemental.

3 Notice where in your body you are feeling your anger or sadness, or whatever emotion you are experiencing. What mental pictures accompany your emotional state? Investigate your emotions and see how they affect you.

4 Remind yourself that you are not your emotions, and that they are transitory and impermanent. Carry this emotional mindfulness into your daily life.

DO THE DISHES

How can dish-washing be a meditation? The Zen tradition encourages you to perform every action with total one-pointed awareness and attention.

Benefits

- Helps you focus and concentrate on what you are doing

- Transforms ordinary chores into a spiritual practice

- Teaches everyday mindfulness

Meditation

When

Practise after any meal, when it is time to wash the dishes.

Preparation

Create dirty dishes by having a nice meal. Clear the table and scrape off the leftover food. Fill your kitchen sink with warm soapy water. Get your scrubbers or dishcloths ready. Roll up your sleeves.

Practice

1 Send everyone out of the kitchen so you can do the dishes alone.

2 Slowly pick up your first dish and begin washing it. Focus exclusively on the dish and the sink. If thoughts intervene, return your focus to what you are doing. When the dish is clean, slowly and mindfully place it in the dish drainer. Pick up your next dish and continue in the same manner.

You may have some difficulty paying such close and undivided attention to washing your dishes at first. You may feel bored because you are accustomed to using dishwashing time to think about other things, or to listen to the radio in the background. If you can transcend your initial boredom, you will reap the joys of mindfulness.

3 Your mind may stray, but try to stay in the present and the task at hand. Notice the movement of the water, the soap suds and the comforting warmth of the water on your hands as you rinse a plate. Notice the dishes, the glasses and pots. Approach the experience as if it is the very first time you have ever washed the dishes.

4 Even though it will take much longer than usual, wash every item in this manner. Although exaggerated, try to bring this level of awareness and deliberate attention to everything you do. Keep your mind present and engaged. Notice if you feel more relaxed and peaceful approaching your life in this way.

SHOPPING

Yes, it is possible to meditate while shopping. It is a good place to become mindful of what you project onto objects.

Benefits

- Demonstrates that acquiring things does not bring happiness
- Promotes mindfulness of motivations for consumption
- Cuts down addiction to shopping and buying

It is easy to assume that external objects are a key to our lasting happiness since that is what advertising tells us constantly. 'Buy this car and feel incredibly powerful!', 'Wear this suit and become a company director overnight!'. We're all susceptible to this kind of pitch because we're all hurting inside in some way, and want to believe that something outside ourselves will take away the pain. But it is time to investigate the issue for ourselves.

Meditation

When

Try this meditation when you are obsessed with buying things that you think will make you happy.

Preparation

Go to a shopping centre alone without money or a credit card. This visit is for meditation only.

Practice

1 As you walk down the rows of shops notice the things that you would like to have. Ask yourself why you want that dress, jacket or car. Do you think it will make you feel better about yourself, perhaps more sexy or attractive? If you buy that jacket and wear it, what do you think it will say to others about you? What qualities and powers are you projecting on to the jacket?

2 Recall the last thing you really had to have and bought. How do you feel about the item now? Did it deliver all that you hoped it would? Even though you were once obsessed with having it, is it now buried in your closet, forgotten?

3 Contemplate the fact that all external things and experiences are, by their nature, ephemeral, unreliable and subject to change and decay. They can never give you real happiness or heal your feelings of inferiority, loneliness or powerlessness.

4 Begin to assess everything you want to buy in this way. Be sure to enjoy your possessions for what they are, but don't project onto them more than they can deliver.

COMPASSIONATE CONSUMPTION

It is important to be aware of what we buy and what resources we consume for the quality of our own lives, for the rest of the planet and for the welfare of future generations.

Benefits

- Reminds us of the interconnectedness of all beings and things

- Provides an antidote to mindless consumption

- Promotes purchase of less toxic products for the benefit of the planet

This meditation is an analytical meditation, one in which you meditate on a topic and try to bring any realizations you have into your daily life. It is not meant to make you feel guilty, and there are no 'shoulds' to be inferred from the practice below. Simply becoming more conscious of your interconnectedness with all others will help you to make more compassionate choices regarding all aspects of your consumption.

Meditation

When

Try this analytical meditation any time you are feeling your buying and spending are out of control.

Preparation

Roughly write down how you have spent your money over the last six months, including energy resources such as fuel for your car.

Practice

1 Sit on you own, on a cushion or a chair. Visualize yourself as connected to all other living beings, to the sky above, the Earth below, the rocks, water, trees and plants. Try to strengthen this feeling of interdependence and connectedness.

2 Imagine that everything you consume has an effect on every other being on Earth. Visualize filling up the tank in your car. Think of the people who drilled the oil, those who refined it into fuel for your car. Remind yourself that it is a limited resource and that car exhaust pollutes the air.

3 Think of all the people involved in growing, shipping and packaging the food you eat. Think about the pesticides and fertilizers that may have been used to grow it and how that affects our planet.

4 Think of the inexpensive t-shirt you are wearing and reflect that it may have been made by people in a third-world country working long hours for very little pay.

5 Bring this consciousness of the effect your consumption has on the planet to your everyday life, and try to make more compassionate decisions regarding what you buy.

ONLY NOW

There is no guaranteed future and the past is gone, so all that is left is now. Be mindful of the present and you will be able to live a happier, richer, more fulfilled life.

Benefits

- Reduces worry and anxiety
- Increases happiness
- Helps you fully inhabit the present moment

Inhabiting the present moment means that you inhabit your life more fully. Being able to take in the sensual richness all around you expands and enriches your experience of life. If you are constantly ruminating about old hurts or planning what you are gong to say in that meeting tomorrow, you will miss being fully alive right now. In reality, right now is all there is, and all you really have.

Meditation

When

Try this if you find yourself stuck in a loop, going over old interactions with friends, family or colleagues, or if you find yourself constantly anticipating what is going to happen tomorrow, next week or next year.

Preparation

For a day, monitor how often your thoughts take you to the past or the future.

Practice

1 Sit on a cushion or a chair and keep your back straight. Focus on your breath for a few minutes to centre yourself. When thoughts intervene, notice if they are thoughts about the future or the past and bring yourself back to the present.

2 Stay in the present by focusing on sensual input from your environment as well as what you are feeling physically or emotionally. Notice how your clothing feels against your body, the temperature of the air, the sounds you can hear and the taste in your mouth. Do you feel sad, lonely or anxious?

3 Relax into your environment. Tell yourself it is OK to just be yourself, exactly as you are, with all your faults and good qualities. No matter what problems you have, you don't have to worry about them. No matter what happened in your past, you can let it go. Experience the present moment becoming richer and more three-dimensional. Breathe in the beauty of now.

4 Try to inhabit the present moment in this way throughout your daily life.

ONE THING AT A TIME

Time-management specialists encourage multi-tasking, but in the long run it is stressful and inefficient. Learn to focus on one task at a time and give it all your loving attention.

Benefits

- Provides a more relaxed way to work
- Helps you stay in the present moment
- Prevents mistakes and accidents

Underlying multi-tasking there is often a competitive and aggressive motivation. In other words, if you get more done in less time, it means you are smarter, more competent and more successful. You may get more done but you never really focus on anything. The quality of your work and your life suffers. Try this meditation to get in touch with the negative effects of multi-tasking and the positive benefits of working on one thing at a time.

Meditation

When

Do this meditation when you are feeling stress as a result of multi-tasking at work or at home.

Preparation

If you usually do more than one thing at a time, ask yourself why you do that.

Practice

1 Pick any task, such as typing or cooking, then do something else as well. Cook dinner and watch TV at the same time. If you are at work, file your documents while making a business call. Write down how you feel and how you performed your tasks.

2 Do the same tasks over again, only this time concentrate on one task only. Cook mindfully and give your full attention to your business call. Write down how you feel and how you performed your tasks.

3 Later, sit on a cushion or chair and recall how you felt while multi-tasking. Try to recreate mentally how you feel when frantically trying to do many things at once. Stay with your feelings for a few minutes. Then recall how you felt when you devoted your total attention to a single task and stay with this feeling for a few minutes.

4 If you felt better focusing on one thing at a time, continue to approach all your tasks in this way. You may notice, over time, that your work will be more precise and well done, and you will feel more relaxed, centred and in control of your life.

THE EYES HAVE IT

Looking deeply into another person's eyes can be a wonderful meditative experience. If you feel you have been taking your partner or a friend for granted, or feel less close than you would like, try this healing meditation.

Benefits

• Opens your heart

• Dissolves defences

• Promotes intimacy and better communication

Meditation

When

If you are feeling you would like to be closer to someone, try this meditation for two.

Preparation

Find a partner who is willing to try this with you for the purpose of helping you feel closer to one another.

Practice

1 Sit cross-legged on cushions or on chairs, facing your partner, with your knees touching. Allow your hands to rest in your lap.

2 Both of you take a few deep breaths to focus and centre yourselves. Begin to look directly into the eyes of your partner. You may want to giggle at first, but understand that this is just nervousness. Let yourself get past that.

3 Spend five minutes looking into each other's eyes. Try not to think. Just take in this other

Sometimes this exercise can be challenging, as you may feel exposed and vulnerable, especially you have been having difficulties with your meditation partner. But if you can stay with it, love will prevail. After all, you both want happiness and you both want to avoid suffering. You have this base in common and can work from there.

human being. If emotions come up, let them. If you want to cry, do; if you want to smile and laugh, do. But let the reaction come from a deep feeling of connection rather than a defence against it.

4 End your meditation by giving each other a hug. If you want to tell your partner anything, you can. It is also fine to stay silent.

MEDIA MONITOR

If you watch TV, listen to the radio, go to movies, read newspapers and books, surf the Internet or play computer games, you are absorbing a great deal of information. Learn to be mindful of what you take in.

Benefits

- Reduces stress from information-overload

- Retrieves lost time from media addiction

- Helps you become mindful of what you take in

The content of what you take in, your motivation for watching or listening and the amount you take in, all have an enormous effect on you. Is your media intake helping or harming you? It is important to examine all three aspects of your media intake, and make clear decisions about how much and what you will allow in your life.

Meditation

When

If you feel you are taking in too much information and are not discriminating enough about what you watch, listen to or read, then try this meditation.

Preparation

For two or three days, keep track of how much time you spend watching TV, surfing the Internet or engaging with other forms of media. Note the content of what you take in. How much is violent or disturbing in nature?

Practice

1 Sit on a chair or cushion in a quiet room away from others. Call to mind some images from any media you have read, viewed or listened to over the past few days.

2 Note how this material makes you feel, what emotions are stirred and how your body is reacting. Is your heart beating faster or are any of your muscles tensing up?

3 Ask yourself if the material you took in is positive and helpful in nature or does it provoke negative emotions such as fear or anger. For instance, if you watched a story about a murder on the evening news, what effect did this have on you? If you watched a documentary on birds, how did that effect you?

4 Now ask yourself why you allowed that media into your life? Were you looking for information? Were you trying to understand a news event? Were you bored and looking for excitement? Were you trying to avoid intimacy or run away from problems?

5 After you have answered these questions for yourself, end your meditation. Try to have some consciousness in the future about your media intake. Make a clear decision about what is good for you and what is not.

SPACE CADET

Do you have a tendency to 'space-out' when you feel overwhelmed by problems and responsibilities? Try this meditation to keep you in the present.

Benefits

- Helps you realize when you space out

- Promotes mindfulness of the present moment

- Gets you in touch with your emotions

Meditation

When

Try this meditation if you have difficulty staying aware of what is going on around you, or if you have had an accident because you were not paying attention.

Preparation

Bring to mind instances where you felt being unaware of your surroundings presented a problem for you or those around you.

Practice

1 Stand barefoot on a wooden floor with your feet shoulder-width apart. Keep your spine straight and shoulders level and relaxed. Your arms can hang loosely at your sides, slightly away from your body, as if you are holding an egg under each armpit. Feel your feet on the smooth floor.

2 Keep your eyes open and breathe naturally. Without turning your head try to take in as much as you can through your senses. Notice the colour of the furniture, the

Has anyone ever said to you 'Earth to Sarah' (or whatever your name is) as a little joke to get your attention? The joke is that you are so completely not present that the person has to make contact by radio from Earth to your space ship somewhere. It is as if you are in your own little world, not available to relate to anyone and oblivious to what is around you. You may use this as a defence against what seems too overwhelming. Or you may just have a habit of being 'an absent-minded professor'. Try hanging up your space suit, if you want to live a more mindful and aware life.

shape and textures of objects in the room. Observe the light and the shadows. Notice any smells and feel the temperature. Now pay attention to any sounds. Do you hear the sound of a fan or the motor humming in your refrigerator?

3 Meditate in this way for ten minutes. If you feel nervous to be this aware, ask yourself why? Practise being this attentive to your environment on a daily basis. Then try being this attentive to people you are with.

LIFE IS SHORT

Your life actually goes by in the blink of an eye. Ask any person who is in their eighties or nineties, and they will almost always tell you to make the best of your time.

Benefits

- Wakes you up to the reality of your death
- Helps you set priorities
- Encourages you to live life to the fullest

This may sound morbid, but it is actually about helping you live fully. If you talk to someone who has recovered from a life-threatening illness, they will often tell you how grateful they are to have had the disease, as it 'woke them up' to the preciousness of life. They may begin to do things they always wanted to do but never got around to. They may quit their job and find another, or end a relationship that ended in spirit a long time ago. Meditating on the fact that you may die at any time, not just in old age, will help you set your priorities and act on them.

Meditation

When

Meditate on the shortness of life if you are feeling emotionally stuck and uninspired.

Preparation

Read the obituaries in your local paper for today. This may sound unappealing but it is very helpful to do this once in a while.

Practice

1 Sit on a cushion or chair in a quiet place where you can be alone.

2 Note your age and how many years you think you can expect to live. Now imagine how you would feel if you knew you were going to die in about two years from now. What would you do differently with your life?

3 Now think about how precious your life is. Who would you want to tell that you loved them? What would you want to do with your remaining time? Would you want to get closer to your family or your friends? Would you quit your job and travel?

4 After about ten minutes, write down everything you imagined you would do. Make doing these things a priority in your life today.

HEALING BODY, MIND AND SPIRIT

HEALING MEDITATIONS

By learning to calm and centre yourself, and practise mindfulness, you have had a taste of the latent powers of your mind. In this section you will learn to use visualization to overcome illness and psychological distress, as well as prevent disease and promote longevity.

As you live, you develop negative habits, such as addictions to food or alcohol, which harm you physically and spiritually. Healing requires letting go of negative habits and replacing them with healthy ones.

So it is appropriate that the first meditation in this section is 'Purifying fire', in which you are invited to literally burn up your negative habits. Unexpressed grief harms the body and soul; in '49 days' you are introduced to a Tibetan Buddhist meditation for working with grief. If you are not getting enough sleep, try 'Sweet dreams' to help you sleep like a baby. If you have addictions, approach them in the most compassionate way with 'Feed your demons'. Being rigid in your approach to life causes untold stress. Learn to relax in the grey zone with 'Hold the opposites'. Harness the power of visualization for healing with the 'Nectar washing' meditation. 'Body scan' teaches a do-it-yourself method for monitoring your health. Enlist the wisdom and strength of trees for healing with 'Great tree meditation'. Your voice is a powerful tool for healing, as you will discover in 'Healing through toning'. If you are pregnant you may want to try 'Good birth'.

For purifying past negative behaviour, try 'Four powers' and 'Making amends'. For deep, healing relaxation try 'Savasana'. To help you prepare for surgery try 'Surgery', and to prevent the need for surgery, heal your organs with a Chinese Taoist meditation called 'Inner smile'.

The three Tara meditations will introduce you to a Tibetan Buddhist female Buddha who specializes in healing and longevity. 'Nourishment' helps you heal from food addiction while 'Patience' teaches the antidote to anger. Learn to be a good parent for yourself and your children in 'Inner child' and 'Best parent'. If you are a caregiver, support yourself with 'Caregiver'. 'Yoni' helps you heal from sexual abuse. 'Rejoicing' helps you transform jealousy. If you have trouble with alcohol addiction try 'Spirit cures spirit'. Finally, give your body a powerful tune up with another Chinese Taoist meditation called 'Microcosmic orbit'.

PURIFYING FIRE

If you have bad habits that affect your mental, emotional, physical or spiritual health, this meditation will help you let go of them and start anew.

Benefits

- Helps you identify how you are harming yourself

- Encourages you to let go of shame or guilt

- Supports you in efforts to care for yourself

Meditation

When

Healing is not just for physical illness. Try this if you are struggling with negative habits.

Preparation

Locate a place where you can safely build a fire – in a fireplace or outside, perhaps in a barbecue. Write down any negative habits you have had in the past or have presently. Take your time and be as thorough as possible. Then write down any feelings you have about your negative habits. Include any shame or regret.

Practice

1 Build a fire in your fireplace or barbecue. Sit on a meditation cushion or a chair nearby. Read your list. Review everything and feel your shame and regret.

2 Visualize your higher power in any form you like. Express your regret for indulging in negative habits and ask for help in living your life in a more positive and constructive way. Feel your

No one is free of negative, undermining habits. It could be that you smoke or you spend too much money or you have a habit of blowing up in anger at your children when you really don't want to. Maybe you drive too fast and have had a few accidents, nearly harming someone. Perhaps you have consistently cheated on your partner. You may still be caught up in your bad habits or you may have given them up, but carry shame about them. This mediation uses visualization to help you overcome negative habits.

higher power's love and acceptance of you as you are.

3 Now place your list into the fire and watch it burn. As your list burns, visualize your negative habits leaving you. Let go of any shame by mentally giving it to the fire to be purified. Commit to living a more positive life.

49 DAYS

Tibetan Buddhists believe in reincarnation. When someone dies, it is understood he or she will spend up to 49 days in transit to the next life. During this time you grieve for them and also pray that they have a good rebirth.

Benefits

- Helps the grieving process
- Gives you hope they will have another life
- Encourages you to live your own life well

You may have experienced the death of someone in your family or perhaps you have lost a good friend. This meditation helps you grieve and send your loved one on to the next life. If you don't believe in reincarnation, don't worry. You can simply think of them in heaven or with God or however you think of an afterlife. If you don't believe in an afterlife, use this meditation to help yourself heal in the 49 days following their death.

Meditation

When

Practise this meditation during and up to 49 days after the death of a loved one.

Preparation

Find a photograph of the person and place it in a frame that can stand on your altar or on a table.

Practice

1 Sit on a cushion or chair in front of your altar or small table on which you have placed the photograph of your loved one.

2 Think of your loved one and let your grief pour out. Cry as much as you need to. Express how much you appreciated and will miss them. When you can, begin to think about their spirit and affirm to yourself that he or she will live on in some form.

3 If you believe in reincarnation, imagine your loved one taking a wonderful rebirth. Pray that the person will have a wonderful new life where he or she will continue to progress on a spiritual path. Mentally release your loved one to a new life. If you feel that the person will be in heaven with God, visualize the person there.

4 If you don't believe in an afterlife, remember the good aspects of your departed loved one and visualize letting him or her go. Release yourself from any guilt or sadness. Visualize your loved one's best quality and try to bring that quality into your life as a way to remember him or her.

SWEET DREAMS

Sleep deprivation is a serious health problem in our overly busy, stress-filled world. If you have trouble sleeping, try this meditation to help you relax and ready yourself for bed.

Benefits

- Helps clear your mind
- Induces relaxation
- Strengthens your immune system

Meditation

When

If you are having trouble getting to sleep, try this simple meditation to help you relax.

Preparation

Prepare yourself for bed.

Practice

1 Make sure your bedroom is quiet. Get into bed and turn off the lights. Ensure that your curtains or shades are pulled closed to keep out any lights from the street.

2 Stretch out on your back and get comfortable. Tense up your body as much as you can and then relax. Repeat three times.

3 Slowly breathe into your lower abdomen 20 times.

If you are like most people, you get seven or eight hours of sleep a night – if you are lucky. Experts suggest that you need a minimum of eight to nine to be at your best physically and mentally. As well as not getting enough sleep, you may have insomnia, or at least difficulty falling asleep. Stress and late-night television can leave you simultaneously wide-awake and exhausted. Over time, getting less sleep than you need will harm your immune system, leaving you vulnerable to illness.

4 Now with each in-breath, breathe in peace, and with each out-breath, breathe out the cares of your day. Release your worries and welcome pleasant dreams. Ask that your dreams be helpful. Surrender to deep relaxation as you let go more and more. Feel yourself sinking into a deep, healing and rejuvenating sleep.

TAP AWAY

There are many new therapeutic techniques for dealing with stress based on tapping opposite sides of your body. This one is simple and forms the basis of a powerful meditation.

Benefits

- Provides a simple method for stress reduction

- Removes stress so you can better deal with problems

- Promotes self-care

This meditation is based on something called Eye Movement Therapy (EMT). Researchers have discovered that moving your eyes from one side to the other while thinking of a traumatic event significantly reduced anxiety and stress. Simply tapping both sides of your body, alternately in a continuous fashion for three minutes or more can have the same effect.

Meditation

When

Practise this technique whenever you are suffering anxiety caused by something in your past or something you are currently worried about.

Preparation

Bring to mind some event, person or situation that has provoked feelings of anxiety and distress.

Practice

1 Sit in a straight-backed chair with your back straight and your hands resting on your thighs.

2 Think about the cause of your anxiety. Visualize as clearly as possible the event, people or situation and fully feel your distress.

3 Now using your index finger, begin to tap lightly, first one thigh then the other, alternating back and forth. Do this rhythmically, at a speed that feels comfortable to you, and that you can sustain for three minutes or more. As you tap, keep visualizing the source of your stress.

4 After three minutes you should feel a lessening of your anxiety. If the anxiety is still partially there, repeat the exercise another time. If it is not completely gone after the second exercise, try again, only this time move your eyes from side to side.

FEED YOUR DEMONS

If you suffer from addictions – drugs, alcohol, food, sex, Internet or whatever – you are probably running away from pain and not nurturing yourself in appropriate ways. Try this meditation to learn how to take better care of yourself.

Benefits

- Helps you heal from addictions
- Promotes self-care
- Heals shame

Because we are creatures of habit, most of us have some kind of addiction. You may have a harmless addiction to blueberries or a more serious one such as recreational or prescription drugs, alcohol or sex. You become addicted to avoid something. It may be to avoid feeling emotions that are painful to you, or to bury disappointments or wounding from your childhood. You may think of your addictions as demons to be exorcized, but try thinking of them as friends who are acting out because they are feeling uncared for and ignored.

Meditation

When

Try this meditation to begin healing from your troublesome addictions.

Preparation

Write a list of all your addictions.

Practice

1 Sit on a meditation cushion or straight-backed chair in a quiet, private place.

2 Bring to mind what you consider to be your most troublesome addiction. Now see your addiction as a person other than yourself. For instance, if your addiction is to cigarettes, you might see your addiction as a thin, sallow-skinned man who is tense and hunched over.

3 Ask the person you have created what he is feeling and what he needs that he is not getting. Your smoking character might tell you he wants to relax, clear his lungs and quit racing all the time.

4 After you have had a conversation with your 'demon' imagine you are responsible for their care and visualize helping them heal. Think of at least one way you could help them feel better and stop abusing themselves. Now apply this nurturing solution to your own life.

HOLD THE OPPOSITES

You may find yourself locked into dualistic thinking – everything has to be right or wrong, black or white, good or bad. This meditation helps you learn to tolerate a more realistic view – that two seemingly opposite points of view or situations can exist simultaneously.

Benefits

- Reduces stress
- Helps you to accept things as they are
- Provides an antidote to rigid thinking

Meditation

When

If you find yourself angry and fearful, wanting simplistic, clear answers or demanding that things be done 'your way', try this meditation to help you tolerate life as it really is.

Preparation

Think about conflict situations where you feel the issues are black and white.

Practice

1 Sit on your meditation cushion or chair in a quiet place where you can be alone. Meditate by watching your breath for about five minutes.

2 Think of a situation where you have been miserable because you wanted something to be a certain way and the other person wanted another outcome. Pay attention to your emotions. The first one to arise may be anger. Check to see if underneath the anger you feel fear. What do you think you will lose if you let both points of view exist simultaneously?

Dualistic thinking is simplistic and is often driven by fear. It cannot contain or express the complexity of life. If your tendency is to think of issues as either black or white, your life will be more stressful and difficult, because the real world is a continuum of greys rather than one of stark contrasts. For example, you may be in conflict with your partner because you think he or she is wrong and you are right. If you want to feel more comfortable on a day-to-day basis, this meditation will help you soften and learn to see that life's answers are much more ambiguous than 'yes' or 'no'.

3 Imagine that you are alone on a desert island with that person and your survival depends on both of you having your needs met. Imagine a creative way to compromise so that each of you has at least part of what you desire.

4 After you have reached your compromise solution where both you and the other person can be 'right' and have something of what you want, notice if you feel less stress and more contentment.

ECTAR WASHING

Visualization is a powerful tool for healing body, mind and spirit.
Use this meditation to ward off illness and promote good health.

Benefits

- Promotes good health
- Prevents illness
- Promotes longevity

The content of your thoughts can have a dramatic effect on the health of your body. If you have an illness and, out of fear, constantly visualize your illness progressing, you are sending a message to the diseased cells to continue with the disease process. If you consciously imagine your body healing, you will support your body in getting well.

When you visualize during meditation, you consciously create images or scenes in your mind. In this meditation you will be asked to visualize a beautiful healing image.

Meditation

When

Try this meditation if you are ill. This is also a wonderful meditation to practise on a regular basis for maintaining your good general health.

Preparation

Sit down for a few minutes and write down any health problems you have, however small or serious.

Practice

1 Sit on a cushion or chair in your usual meditation space. Begin by watching your breath for a few minutes.

2 Think of all the health problems you listed. See them as black spots residing in various parts of your body. Note how your health problems hinder your life, feel any emotions that arise.

3 Visualize that you are near a beautiful waterfall in a warm, tropical location. No one is around. Undress and find a place where you can sit directly under the flow. Imagine that the water is not ordinary water, but a heavenly nectar that heals illness and prevents disease.

4 Visualize all your health problems being cleansed by this nectar. Feel the nectar not only flowing over your body but through it as well, taking with it all the black spots you visualized earlier.

5 Affirm to yourself that your body is now free of health problems. Get up from your seat under the waterfall, dry off and put on your clothes. Leave this beautiful site knowing that you are in vibrant health. Know that you can return to it whenever you want.

BODY SCAN

It is important to pay attention to your body on a regular basis and monitor any signs of imbalance. This meditation will help you take responsibility for your health.

Benefits

- Keeps you in good communication with your body
- Promotes self-care
- Promotes relaxation

You may be one of those people who is only conscious of your body from the head up. You may forget you have a body! This mediation will teach you a powerful technique that helps you pay attention to subtle changes in your body – changes that could signal imbalance and the beginning of more serious problems.

Meditation

When

Practise this short meditation on a regular basis if possible.

Preparation

Do some stretching exercises to bring feeling and awareness to your body as a whole.

Practice

1 Stretch out on a mat or on your bed with no pillow, with your arms comfortably extended from your body, palms up. Cover yourself with a light blanket if you think you might get chilled. Breathe naturally into your lower abdomen for about 20 breaths. Relax any tense areas of your body.

2 Begin at your toes, slowly working your way up your body, and notice any discomfort along the way. Ask yourself if you have had any pain, twinges or unusual sensations in the recent past. Ask that any problems you might have, be made known to you, even if you have been ignoring symptoms. If you discover an area that needs attention, such as your back, your stomach or liver, mentally take note.

3 When you reach the crown of your head, end your body scan. Relax for a few minutes, then sit up and write down any problems you may have discovered. If you feel they could be serious, see your health practitioner. Or you may decide you need a better diet or some exercise. Over time, this practice can help you stay in tune with your body and its needs.

MANDALA DRAWING

Mandala is a Sanskrit word for 'sacred circle'. Native American, Hindu and Buddhist cultures have used mandala drawing for healing and spiritual development.

Benefits

- Promotes healing, psychological and spiritual integration

- Helps uncover hidden emotions

- Enhances creativity

A mandala, either painted or drawn, is a circular symbol of the universe that uses symmetrical shapes, often divided into four, focused around the centre. It symbolizes the elements, the four directions, and the stars and planets. When you look at a mandala it gives you a view into a sacred space, vibrating with wholeness and balance. In nature you can find mandalas in flowers, fruit and snow crystals. The mandala drawings you create symbolize you: your body, your psychological state and your place in the world.

Meditation

When

Create a mandala whenever you want to explore something in yourself that is hidden or if you want to heal past wounds.

Preparation

Gather together the art materials you would like to use. Use a plate or compass to draw the circle.

Practice

1 Make sure you are in a quiet, private space. Light a candle or burn incense to create a reflective mood. Focus on the emotion, subject or pain you want to express in your mandala.

2 Draw a circle either by freehand, with a compass or trace around a plate. Fill in the circle with colour and form. Allow your mandala to unfold. Whatever you create is fine; there is no right or wrong mandala.

3 When you have finished, look at your mandala and write down what the colours, form and images mean to you. Perhaps you used yellows and reds, and drew an animal or a person, or you favoured blues and whites. Place your mandala where you can see it often, and let it be part of your life for a time. Be open to receive any messages that it has for you.

GREAT TREE MEDITATION

This is a wonderful meditation for regaining strength after an illness. Let the tree support you in your journey back to health.

Benefits

- Connects you with the Earth element
- Reassures in times of stress
- Strengthens your intention to regain vitality

Trees are a treasured source of energy for practising meditation. The solidity of a tree – its roots connect it with the energy of the Earth – is a quality that helps you heal body and soul. If trees survive humans, insects and disease, they can live a very long time; some for hundreds, even thousands of years.

Meditation

When

Practise this meditation any time you are recovering from an illness or an extended period of stress, preferably at dawn or dusk when the energies of trees are most available.

Preparation

Locate an area that has trees growing in it where you can have some privacy.

Practice

1 Walk slowly through the trees without focusing on any single tree. Wait for one tree to select you by suddenly becoming the attractive focus of your attention in a way that differs from all the surrounding trees.

2 Stand facing or away from the tree trunk, depending on the size of the tree and your personal preference. If it is a small tree, you may be able to partially encircle the trunk with your arms without actually touching it. A larger tree may ask you to stand with your back as close to it as possible without actually making physical contact.

3 Relax by feeling yourself breathing with the tree. Feel every part of your body gently expand and contract as you inhale and exhale naturally, smoothly and softly. Experience the feeling that there is no difference between you and the tree.

4 Sit down with your back against the tree trunk and close your eyes. Imagine the trunk is your own spine, and through it tremendous energy is being transmitted into your body. Continue as long as you are comfortable.

5 Now mentally return to your own body and thank your chosen tree for its support.

HEALING THROUGH TONING

Toning is a powerful approach to healing yourself through the use of your voice. It is a vocal healing meditation that can help you free your natural voice and connect with the vibrations of your body.

Benefits

- Releases tension
- Uplifts the spirit
- Heals the body

When toning you 'sing' sustained, vocalized tones that resonate in your body. Through toning, you vibrate and stimulate your entire physical system. You literally tone your body, which helps regulate blood flow, increases oxygenation and heals the nervous system, glands and organs.

Meditation

When

Practise toning when you want
to energize or heal both your
body and spirit.

Preparation

Find a place where you can be alone and out of
earshot of others.

Practice

1 Stand with your feet well grounded
and your shoulders and arms relaxed.
Begin to hum into your centre; it may be
your lower abdomen or your heart area.
Gradually feel your hum expand
throughout your entire body. Hum into
your bones, muscles and internal organs.

2 Allow your hum to open gradually
into a full-voiced sound or tone, and
continue to feel it resonating throughout
your whole body.

3 Ask what needs to be healed.
Visualize any toxins being expelled
through your feet. Continue toning into
any area of your body needing release or
healing. Make any sounds you want. Let
them arise spontaneously. Imagine that
your toning is connected with the
vibrations of the entire universe.

4 When you feel ready, end your
toning mediation. Stand quietly for
a moment and affirm that your body is
completely healed and rejuvenated.

GOOD BIRTH

If you are pregnant, you will want to prepare yourself mentally, emotionally, physically and spiritually for the birth of your child. This meditation will help both you and your baby.

Benefits

- Helps you visualize a healthy birth
- Encourages self-care
- Benefits the child in your womb

Meditation

When

Practise this meditation throughout your pregnancy.

Preparation

Spend some time writing about why you wanted this baby and what kind of parent you would like to be.

Practice

1 Stretch out on your bed or on a mat on the floor. Make yourself comfortable in any way you can, with pillows under your back or knees. Breathe normally for about 20 breaths, calming any anxiety you may have.

2 Place your hands on your lower abdomen and mentally and emotionally connect with your child growing within. Visualize that tiny body and mentally breathe into it, sending peace and calm to him and her so he or she develops into a strong, healthy baby. See your child as serene, beautiful and

If you are giving birth for the first time you may have fears about birth pains or about being a parent for the first time. If you are already a mother, your concerns may be about the stress of taking care of an additional child. Whether you are a first-time mother or not, meditation will enhance your pregnancy and childbirth experience. When you meditate, you not only calm and centre yourself, you also pass on your sense of well-being through the placenta and through sympathetic resonance with your baby. You can also use meditation to consciously communicate with your baby.

joyous. Tell your child that he or she is sacred and has an important place in the universe.

3 Visualize the birth going very smoothly with no difficulties. Imagine holding your newborn baby in your arms and falling instantly in love. Mentally commit to being the best parent you can be for this child.

4 Return to watching your breath. Relax deeply. When you are ready, end your meditation.

FOUR POWERS

Tibetan Buddhists have a wonderful meditation for taking stock of your actions and purifying any negativity you may have caused. Here is a simplified version of the four powers.

Benefits

- Helps you keep track of positive and negative actions

- Purifies negative actions

- Rejuvenates your meditation practice

Buddhist teachers will tell you that everyone generates negative karma every day. It is an inevitable reality of being a human being. For example, you may have told someone a small 'white lie' or you may have done something more harmful such as cheating a client out of money. Those negative actions, whether insignificant or more serious, produce negative karma and benefit from purification on a daily basis.

Meditation

When

This practice is best done at the end of every day before you go to bed, but if you can't manage it then, do it as often as you can.

Preparation

Review your day.

Practice

1 Think of the negative actions you have committed and anyone you may have hurt, directly or indirectly. Consider the most insignificant act to the more serious. Generate a feeling of compassion for those you have harmed.

2 Generate a sincere feeling of regret. This should not be senseless guilt or self-recrimination. Simply recognize that your negative actions were very unwise for yourself and others.

3 Promise not to repeat these negative actions. It is good if you can promise to avoid a negative behaviour for a specific time, or at least promise that you will make an effort to avoid repeating the behaviour.

4 Commit to an action you can perform in the future as an antidote to your negativity. This could be doing something positive for someone you harmed. You can use any positive action with a good motivation; it doesn't have to involve the person you harmed. For instance, you could read a spiritual text for inspiration to help you live a more positive life.

5 After you have completed the 'four powers' end your meditation by affirming that you have purified your negativity for the past day.

MAKING AMENDS

One way to clean house mentally and free yourself of baggage from your past is to make amends to those you may have harmed. Sincerely expressing your regret will unburden your mind and heart and possibly heal your relationships.

Benefits

- Promotes psychological healing
- Dissolves anger
- Encourages personal responsibility

The psychological burden of unexpressed regret can take its toll on your body and your psychological well-being. To heal body and mind, consider making amends for past harmful actions. If you feel it is appropriate, express regret directly to a person you have harmed. If you feel you will create more negativity by contacting them, 'confess' and express your regret to someone else you trust.

The meditation opposite will help you prepare to do either one.

Meditation

When

Try this meditation if you feel burdened by guilt and remorse because you have harmed others in the past.

Preparation

List the people you have harmed, what you did to harm them and your motivation for doing so. For example, you may have used an affair with a supervisor at work in order to get a promotion. Be fearless and thorough in your inventory.

Practice

1 Sit on a cushion or chair in front of your altar or sacred space. Light a candle. If you believe in God or a higher power, ask Him or Her for guidance and courage for what you plan to do.

2 Bring to mind the people you have harmed, what you did to harm them and why you did so. Feel sincere regret for what you did.

3 Choose one person you have harmed and write a letter telling them how you harmed them and why you did so. Express your regret and ask for forgiveness.

4 After you have written the letter, visualize your higher power smiling at you while looking on with love and compassion. Feel the warmth of His or Her acceptance and support in making amends with the person you harmed.

5 Decide whether you are going to contact the person or let your letter suffice. After you have made your decision, feel your guilt evaporate. Generate good wishes, love and compassion for the person. End your meditation session.

SAVASANA

One of the most healing and restorative yoga postures is called *savasana* or 'corpse pose'. It is the posture of complete relaxation and can be used as a healing meditation for body and mind.

Benefits

- Allows you to let go completely
- Provides an alternative pose for breath meditation
- Rejuvenates body and mind

Practising this pose will reveal just how much stress and tension you carry in your body in everyday life. It is said to stimulate blood circulation, exercise inner organs and alleviate fatigue, nervousness, asthma, constipation, diabetes, indigestion and insomnia.

Meditation

When

Practise this rejuvenating meditation whenever you feel fatigued.

Preparation

Gather a yoga mat, a blanket and an extra pillow to place under your knees.

Practice

1 Lie on your back on a mat, where you will not be disturbed. Place a pillow under your knees and cover yourself with a blanket. Let your arms relax, palms up, at your side. Keep your heels slightly apart. Breathe slowly and deeply, feeling a sense of calm relaxation come over your whole body.

2 Slowly inhale through your nostrils and tense your ankles, feet and toes. Hold your breath while you tighten your muscles. Exhale and relax. Slowly inhale and contract your kneecaps, calves, ankles, feet and toes. Hold and tighten. Exhale and relax.

3 Slowly inhale, contracting all the muscles of your abdomen, pelvic area, thighs, kneecaps, calves, ankles, feet and toes. Hold your breath and tighten the muscles. Exhale and relax.

4 Inhale. Tense your neck, shoulders, arms and elbows, wrists, hands and fingers, chest muscles, down to the toes. Hold and tense. Exhale and relax. Inhale and contract your scalp and the muscles of your face. Tighten your tongue, constrict your throat and tighten your whole body. Now let your stress and tension melt into the floor.

5 Meditate by watching your breath for five minutes more.

SURGERY

You want to be in the best possible mental space when you have surgery. This meditation will help you prepare.

Benefits

- Calms anxiety

- Improves mental state before surgery

- Encourages a good outcome

Meditation

When

If you have surgery scheduled, practise this meditation every day, several times a day, leading up to the surgery.

Preparation

Keep a journal in the days leading up to surgery, writing down your thoughts, fears and hopes for recovery.

Practice

1 If you are well enough, sit on a meditation cushion or a chair. If not, it is fine to do this meditation while reclining in bed. Begin by watching your breath for ten minutes. Breathe deeply into your lower abdomen.

2 Visualize the part of your body requiring surgery. See the illness or damage that needs to be repaired. Visualize healing light infusing the entire area, beginning the healing process even before surgery takes place.

If you are anxious and worried in the days leading up to your surgery, this meditation practice can help, by calming your mind and utilizing visualization to encourage a positive experience. A calm mind enhances your immune system and chances for recovery. If the imagery is not right for you, feel free to change it to suit your needs.

3 Next, see your surgeon as a white knight wielding his sword, vanquishing the illness that is causing you so much distress. Visualize your body bathed in healing light as the surgeon skilfully finishes his work.

4 Imagine yourself after surgery, strong and able to handle any discomfort well because your body is on its way back to health and vitality. Stay with this image and feeling as long as you like and when you are ready, close your meditation.

INER SMILE

The 'inner smile' is a gentle tool used by Taoist practitioners to enhance health and well-being. It helps you give your internal body the loving attention it deserves.

Benefits

- Promotes awareness of your internal body and organs
- Prevents illness
- Promotes healing

Meditation

When

Practise the inner smile at any time, anywhere, on a daily basis. Wait an hour after eating to begin your meditation.

Preparation

Read an anatomy book to understand where your organs are in your body.

Practice

1 Sit comfortably near the edge of a chair with feet flat on the floor. Visualize a source of smiling energy about a metre (three feet) in front of you. This can be an image of your own smiling face or of someone or something you love and respect.

2 Let the smiling energy accumulate between your eyebrows. Allow it to flow down from your mid-eyebrow through your face and down your neck. Let it flow down to your thymus gland, which is located behind your sternum. Picture it glowing with vibrant health.

3 Feel the stream of smiling energy flow down into your heart. Let it relieve stored tension. Radiate the love from your heart to your lungs. Feel your lungs breathe with ease. Now smile into your liver on the right side, just below the rib cage. If your liver is hard, soften it with your smile.

4 Let the smiling energy flow across your abdomen to your pancreas, which is located within the left lower rib-cage. Thank it for its work and see that it is healthy and functioning smoothly.

5 Continuing to the left, smile into your spleen. Thank it for its hard work. Direct the smile to your kidneys, in your lower back just below the rib-cage on either side of the spine. The adrenal glands sit on top of them. Smile at your adrenals, and you may feel a burst of adrenalin. Finally, send the smiling energy into your urinary tract, bladder, urethra and genitals.

6 End by storing the smiling energy in your navel area, about 3 cm (1½ in) inside your body.

\RA I

This beautiful meditation is the first of three based on a Tibetan Buddhist meditation on Tara, the female manifestation of the Buddha. It will help you heal from fear in its many forms.

Benefits

- Heals you from fear
- Promotes compassion for yourself
- Reduces negative emotions

You may think of fear as simply the state of being frightened. For example, if your small child runs ahead of you towards a busy street, you will feel fear. But, fear is often the emotional state of mind at the root of your negative emotions. Tibetan Buddhists meditate on the female Buddha Tara to help transform these negative emotional states. You don't have to be a Buddhist to practise this meditation.

Meditation

When

Practise this meditation when you want to get to the root of your troublesome emotions.

Preparation

Think about how fear can be the cause of your difficult emotions.

Practice

1 Sit on a cushion or chair in meditation posture. Breathe in deeply and exhale slowly ten times to focus and concentrate your mind. Now visualize a beautiful female Buddha seated in meditation posture in front of you. Notice that she is very kind, compassionate and patient. Ask her to help remove your fears that manifest themselves in the form of negative emotions.

2 If, out of fear that you will be abandoned, you are controlling with your loved ones, ask Tara that you be able to practise unconditional love. If you have fear that manifests in anger because you are afraid you are going to be harmed or taken advantage of, ask

Tara to help you feel more confident in your ability to care for yourself, and more patient and tolerant of others.

3 If you have fear that manifests as jealousy, ask Tara to help you rejoice in others' happiness. If your fear causes you to be miserly and withhold yourself or your possessions from others, ask Tara to help you be more generous.

4 Visualize Tara granting your wishes. See her as being available at all times to help and support you in living a more compassionate life.

TARA II

In this second meditation on the female Buddha Tara, you meditate on her for protection.

Benefits

- Helps you set healthy boundaries
- Provides protection and support
- Encourages personal growth

Meditation

When

Try this meditation if you are feeling unprotected and overwhelmed.

Preparation

Spend time observing colours in nature. Appreciate the brilliant colours of flowers and the more subtle shades in a forest.

Practice

1 Sit on a cushion or chair in meditation posture. Now visualize a beautiful female Buddha seated in meditation posture in front of you. Imagine a beautiful translucent white light coming from inside Tara's heart. Let it engulf you and enter your heart. From both your hearts, the light radiates out to form an egg-shaped shield that extends about 1.5 metres (5 feet) from your body in all directions. Imagine that this shield brings peace to your life and your relationships.

2 Visualize a yellow-gold light coming from Tara's heart. It enters yours and extends out forming another shield about 1.5 metres (5 feet) beyond the white shield, protecting you and helping rejuvenate your physical health.

3 Now visualize an orange-red light coming from Tara's heart to yours and then creating another shield extending beyond the white and yellow-gold ones. This shield helps you develop the power to be effective in your work, family and spiritual life.

4 Visualize brilliant blue light coming from Tara's heart creating another shield as above. This shield helps you to set healthy boundaries in your personal and work life.

5 The light from Tara's heart now turns a gorgeous green and creates yet another shield beyond the others you have already created. This green shield helps you to perform the many activities in your life.

6 Visualize the light from Tara's heart turns a rust colour, creating the final shield. This shield stabilizes the others and makes them function. Feel Tara's blessing and thank her for her help. Know that you can go forward in life with renewed energy, confidence and protection.

TARA III

In this third meditation on the female Buddha Tara, you meditate to heal the elements that make up your body.

Benefits

- Heals your physical body
- Strengthens the elements that make up your body
- Promotes longevity

Meditation

When

Practise this third version of White Tara meditation if you are ill or want to prevent illness.

Preparation

Be open to the Tibetan idea that your body is made up of five elements – Earth, Water, Fire, Air and Space.

Practice

1 Sit on your meditation cushion or chair. Now visualize a beautiful female Buddha seated in meditation posture in front of you. Ask her that you be healed from illness or imbalance in your body.

2 Visualize a gold light streaming from Tara's heart, extending throughout the universe gathering all Earth energies, which return to her heart. Her body fills with gold light. From her heart this gold light streams forward into your heart. Your body fills with beautiful gold light, which heals all your organs.

3 The light from Tara's heart now turns white, extends into the universe and gathers all Water energies, and returns to her heart. Her body fills with white light. From her heart the white light streams into your heart. Your body fills with white light and all moisture and fluids that are found in your body are healed, balanced and rejuvenated.

4 In the same manner, the light from Tara's heart now turns red, gathering heat energy from the universe. From her heart red light streams into your heart. Your body fills with red light, healing your digestion and any imbalance there may be in body temperature.

5 The light streaming from Tara's heart now turns green, gathering air energy and returning as above. From her heart green light streams into your heart. Your body fills with green light, healing any respiratory illness.

6 Finally, the light streaming from Tara's heart turns light blue, gathering Space energies, which return to her heart. From her heart, blue light streams into your heart. Your body fills with blue light, healing the spaces in your body that allow your organs, cells and other systems to function effectively.

7 End your meditation by affirming that all your bodily elements have been healed and rejuvenated. Thank Tara for her help and blessing.

NOURISHMENT

Obesity is on the rise as is addiction to food. This meditation helps you to heal the reasons behind this need to over-eat and to learn better ways to nurture your body and soul.

Benefits

- Supports weight loss
- Helps replace food with appropriate nourishment
- Balances relationship to food

You may be over-eating because you are not feeding yourself emotionally. If you really need love and are afraid to give it or ask for it, you may be eating ice cream instead. But that food is a poor substitute for love.

Meditation

When

Try this meditation on a weekly basis if you have a problem with over-eating and excess weight.

Preparation

Write down all the ways that you are not being nourished emotionally, either by yourself or by others.

Practice

1 Sit on a cushion or a straight-backed chair in a quiet, private place. Light a candle and incense if you like.

2 Bring to mind how you felt right before you last over-ate. Even though you may have blocked it at the time, ask yourself what you were feeling? If you were feeling sad, lonely, angry or scared, allow yourself to feel the emotion once again, or perhaps for the first time. Go deeper and ask yourself what caused the emotion. Perhaps you are afraid you will never have a partner, or that the one you have makes you sad because he or she doesn't communicate with you. It could be pain from your childhood.

3 Now imagine other ways you could have helped yourself besides eating food. Maybe you could have admitted your feelings, written them in your journal, taken a hot bath or written a letter to your uncommunicative partner to share later.

4 Feel how you might feel if your real needs were met. Breathe deeply for a few minutes, holding that feeling in mind. End your meditation when you are ready.

PATIENCE

Anger is one of the most destructive emotions for your health. Meditating on its antidote, patience, will make your life more pleasant for you and those around you.

Benefits

- Promotes peace in your relationships
- Encourages tolerance and patience with others
- Reduces stress

In Buddhism, patience means 'forbearance' and refers to that quality of remaining calm in the face of adversity or provocation. Specifically, it means not giving in to your anger. Anger is a strong force within everyone. On a day-to-day level, notice how you can become irritated by the most trivial of things, despite your good nature. The Buddha recommended dealing with anger through meditation in order to become calmer, more aware of emotions and more loving towards others.

Meditation

When

If you feel you have been too angry lately, try this meditation to help you learn patience.

Preparation

Think about when you have been angry recently and what caused your anger.

Practice

1 Sit on a cushion or chair in your meditation space. Practise watching your breath for five minutes to calm and focus your body and mind.

2 Bring to mind the last time you were angry with someone. Are you still angry? If not, where has your anger gone? Ask yourself if getting angry in that situation helped you or hurt you. Ask yourself if it helped you become a kinder, more loving person.

3 Think of how you would feel if you were able to give that person more space to be who they are, regardless of how much they irritate you. Imagine doing that now. Feel the peace that comes over you as you relax and give up the need to fight. Generate a sincere desire for that person to be happy and free of suffering.

4 Come back to the present. Sit watching your breath for another five minutes and end your meditation.

INNER CHILD

Some of us never grew up, not because we were spoilt brats, but because we didn't have adequate parenting. This meditation will help you learn to parent yourself.

Benefits

- Heals family trauma
- Promotes self-nurture
- Strengthens self-regard

Despite their best intentions, your parents may have had difficulties being parents. Perhaps they had difficult childhoods themselves. This meditation is not about assigning blame. Rather, it is about learning to take care of yourself if you were not taught these skills when you were young.

Meditation

When

This is a great meditation if you would like to learn to take better care of yourself both physically and emotionally.

Preparation

Gather a pad of lined paper and a pen.

Practice

1 Sit in meditation posture in a quiet space. Light a candle or incense to help you focus. Meditate on your breath for a few minutes to calm your mind.

2 Divide your pad of paper into two columns. At the top, on the left side, write 'parent', and on the right side write 'child'. Now imagine you are your own parent and ask your child what they are feeling and what they need right now. Write this in the first column.

3 Shift your mental state and become your 'inner child'. From this place, answer your 'parent'. Write as much as you want. Shift back to the parent mind and answer your child. If your child is angry with you as 'parent' ask what you

can do to take care of them. If your child is sad, talk to the child to discover what is at the root of the problem. Have this dialogue in written form for no more than twenty minutes.

4 As 'parent', tell your child that you have had a tough time taking care of him or her, but you would like to be a better parent and have more conversations like this.

5 End your meditation by watching your breath for a few minutes. Notice if you feel calmer and more relaxed.

BEST PARENT

Parenting is the most difficult and important job on the planet.
Try this meditation to help you visualize how to be a better parent.

Benefits

- Helps you be the best parent you can be
- Encourages thinking about parenting
- Promotes easier relationships with your children

Up until recently, parenting was a communal affair. Extended families took the pressure off when you needed a break from your two-year-old, or that rebellious teenager. Now, a great deal is asked of mothers and fathers who parent without the help of aunts, uncles, cousins or grandparents living nearby. Practising this meditation will help you manifest the parent you would like to be on a daily basis.

Meditation

When

If you are a parent, practise this meditation on a weekly basis.

Preparation

Find time to be alone for half an hour. Bring an offering of something like fruit or flowers to your meditation space.

Practice

1 Sit on your meditation cushion or chair. If you have an altar, light a candle. Offer a flower or piece of fruit to your higher power. Make a mental connection with your higher power. If you don't believe in a higher power and don't have an altar, make a mental offering to the highest part of yourself – your best self.

2 Bring to mind the qualities you would like to have as a parent. Your list might include being emotionally available, being supportive and non-judgemental or being able to play with them. You may want to be able to set good boundaries or to know when to protect them and when to encourage them to venture forth. Even if you don't have the skills you want, visualize yourself having them.

3 Ask your higher power to help you become the parent you would like to be. Imagine your higher power smiling at you, accepting you as the parent you are now and offering support and encouragement to be the best parent you can be.

4 End your meditation by sitting quietly for a few minutes, enjoying the peace and quiet.

CAREGIVER

If you are a caregiver for someone who is seriously ill, this meditation will help you care for yourself so you can better care for your loved one. If you are a professional caregiver, this one is for you too.

Benefits

- Rejuvenates you for this difficult work

- Helps you set healthy boundaries

- Helps you process emotions

Meditation

When

Practise this meditation whenever you are feeling overwhelmed by your responsibilities as a caregiver.

Preparation

Acknowledge how you are feeling. Let go of any guilt for taking time for yourself.

Practice

1 Lie down on a mat on the floor or stretch out on your bed. Place both hands over your heart. Breathe into your heart area for a few minutes. Relax as much as you can.

2 Silently acknowledge the qualities that you appreciate about yourself. Acknowledge that you are a very responsible and responsive person. You have the ability to feel deeply for others who are in pain or in need.

Pushing your needs aside, losing your personal boundaries and giving in to self-neglect, exhaustion, apathy and even depression are all potential dangers for any caregiver. Meditation can help alleviate the stresses of your care-giving. This meditation will help you cope with this challenging work.

3 Acknowledge your other strengths and the contributions that you make to your loved one or patients, if you are a professional caregiver. Be sure to acknowledge the love you have given and received.

4 Feel the energy around your heart area expand to fill your whole body. Stay in this position for as long as you like and then end your mediation.

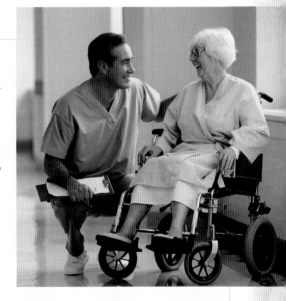

YONI

Yoni is a Sanskrit word meaning 'womb', 'abode' or 'source'. This meditation will help you heal from sexual violation and abuse you have suffered, and allow you to have a positive relationship with your body and your sexuality.

Benefits

- Helps you heal from sexual violation
- Creates positive feelings about sexuality
- Strengthens healthy boundaries

If you have suffered from sexual abuse, you probably have issues with shame. You may have developed negative feelings about your body and your sexuality. Meditation can help you on your journey to recovery.

Meditation

When

Meditate whenever you want help in your healing process.

Preparation

Write three pages in your journal about your body and how you feel about it.

Practice

1 Lie down on a yoga mat on the floor. Cover yourself with a light blanket. Imagine you are taking a journey to a beautiful Goddess temple in another place and another time.

2 A priestess greets you as you arrive at the temple. She tells how the temple door, which is the Goddess's symbolic vulva, was damaged in the last invasion. Although the door has been replaced, there is spiritual damage to be healed. She calls on you to help her, because all women are made in the image of the Goddess and have their own Sacred Doorways.

3 She asks that you put your hands on your body and think about how carefully, how gently, you would want your own doorway to be opened. She goes to the door of the temple and prays to the Goddess with the words 'I love you, please let me in'.

4 Suddenly, the temple door opens a little and you can see the light shining and smell the incense from within. You enter and behold the Goddess. You approach the Goddess and tell her your deepest shame. She receives your shame with love and burns it in a ritual fire. As you leave the sanctuary, you know that you have received a healing deep within yourself that will unfold and manifest itself when the time is right.

LETTING GO, MOVING ON

Benefits

- Helps you have the courage to let go
- Strengthens self-esteem
- Encourages love and respect during separation

Sometimes it is necessary to end your love relationship. This separation is difficult and painful regardless of whether you want it or not. This meditation will help you through.

It takes courage to separate from someone you once never wanted to leave. You may have been deeply in love at one time, yet now you may feel angry, hurt, disappointed and disillusioned. It is natural to want to hang on, because you may not want to face being alone, yet your higher self knows it is time to go. Let meditation support you during this transition.

Meditation

When

Practise when your resolve to end a relationship is shaky, even though you know you should. Try this meditation to help you let go and move on.

Preparation

Find a place to meditate away from the person you are planning to leave.

Practice

1 Sit in meditation posture on your cushion or chair. Meditate on watching your breath for five minutes. Try to calm your body and mind if you have been emotionally distraught.

2 Visualize the person you are leaving in front of you. Tell him or her why you were attracted to them in the beginning and what qualities you admired in him or her at the time. Recall three wonderful times you had together. Thank him or her for the wonderful times that you have shared.

3 Do not discuss your anger or express any negativity. Instead, generate the desire for him or her to be happy in the future. Tell them it will be hard to let go of your relationship, but that you must move on for your own highest good. Imagine your partner agreeing to let you go and wishing you well.

4 If you feel like crying go ahead. Feel strengthened and nurtured by your own positive and loving energy. End your meditation by watching your breath for five minutes.

REJOICING

You may find that when your best friend gets a great job, you feel less than happy for them. In fact, you may feel downright jealous. This meditation helps you transform those sour grapes into champagne.

Benefits

- Helps you transform your jealousy into real joy
- Opens your heart
- Improves your relationships

It may sound difficult to rejoice when someone else gets the job you want or when your difficult neighbour wins the lottery, but it feels so much better than being jealous.

Meditation

When

Try this meditation if ever you feel overcome with jealousy at someone else's good fortune.

Preparation

If you are jealous over something, admit it to yourself. Write a paragraph about why you are jealous.

Practice

1 Sit on a cushion or chair in front of your altar, if you have one, or simply sit in your sacred space.

2 Think about the situation that is making you jealous. Are you jealous because you're feeling possessive of your romantic partner's affections? Are you jealous because a friend received a fantastic inheritance? What brings up jealousy for you?

3 Ask yourself if your jealousy is really serving you. Does is help you get what you want? Is it empowering you? Would the thing or situation you're jealous over really make you that happy? Would your happiness last? Why does a friend's good fortune make you feel bad about yourself?

4 Choose one situation where you are or have been intensely jealous of a friend or work mate. Now rejoice in that person's good fortune. Generate a genuine feeling of generosity towards him or her, and wish them all the best. Feel your self-cherishing lessen and your heart open. Notice that when you rejoice for your friend's good fortune you feel happy and free. You may feel alone, and separate, but you aren't.

5 End your meditation by generating a sense of compassion for yourself and others who struggle with jealousy. Commit to rejoicing whenever you feel jealousy arise.

SPIRIT CURES SPIRIT

If you have a problem with alcohol abuse, the cure involves more than staying away from drink. You need to nurture your soul and reconnect with your spiritual life. This meditation will give you some help on your way.

Benefits

- Supports recovery from alcohol addiction

- Heals your spirit

- Encourages you to rely on a spiritual path

Bill Wilson, the founder of Alcoholics Anonymous (AA), credits Carl Jung with discovering spiritual experience as a cure for alcoholism. The first three steps of the Twelve Steps Program of AA are the following: 1. We admit we are powerless over alcohol – that our lives have become unmanageable; 2. We believe that a Power greater than ourselves can restore us to sanity; and 3. We made a decision to turn our will and our lives over to the care of God as we understand Him [or Her]. The following meditation is inspired by the third step.

Meditation

When

If you are having difficulty using willpower to stop drinking, use this meditation to enlist the help of your higher power to help end your addiction.

Preparation

Assess your drinking and how it is harming you.

Practice

1 Sit on a cushion or chair in your meditation space. Light a candle. Focus on your breath for five minutes to calm and clear your mind.

2 Visualize a warm, loving light around your heart area. Feel this area soften and open.

3 Visualize your higher power seated in front of you. Offer a prayer to them. Ask that you be given assistance on your journey to overcome addiction to alcohol. Pray that your vision be expanded beyond the material world to include the spiritual and sacred realms of reality. Finally, ask that you be able to maintain compassion for yourself during this difficult journey.

4 End your meditation by visualizing your higher power taking up residence in your heart.

MICROCOSMIC ORBIT

This little-known Taoist meditation called the 'Microcosmic Orbit' is a great way to heal your organs and maintain good health.

Benefits

- Keeps your organ systems in balance
- Promotes healing of disease or illness
- Prevents illness

The Microcosmic Orbit meditation is based on the Chinese meridian system of energy channels in your body. Internal energy is circulated via the 'orbit' formed by the Governing Channel meridian which travels from your perineum up to your head, and the Conception Channel meridian which travels from your head back down to perineum. Taoists believe that this meditation fills the Governing and Conception channels with energy, which is then distributed through the organ meridians to all your major organs, energizing and rejuvenating them.

Meditation

When

Practise this any time to keep the energy in your body flowing smoothly.

Preparation

Read the meditation first before trying it to get a feel for the path of the orbit.

Practice

1 Sit on a straight-backed chair with your feet flat on the floor. Calm your mind and regulate your breath. When your mind is settled, turn your attention to your navel. Visualize a pocket of energy glowing in your umbilical region. If it is possible for you, try to feel the energy. Use your mind to guide it down to the perineum and back up through your coccyx.

2 When you feel the energy has gone through this area, visualize it rising up to where your ribs meet your spine. Now, visualize it traveling right up to the base of your skull.

3 When the energy goes through this spot, press the tongue against your palate. Next visualize the energy

reaching your crown. Then focus attention on the spot between your eyebrows and draw energy down from your crown and out through the point between the brows.

4 Let the energy sink down through the spot between your eyebrows, through your palate and tongue into your throat, down to your heart. Draw it down through your solar plexus, into your naval area once again. Repeat the cycle as many times as you wish.

5 End your meditation by affirming that your organs have been healed and rejuvenated.

GET MOVING

MOVING MEDITATIONS

Meditation can be more than sitting on a cushion. Spiritual practitioners from all cultures and all traditions make use of sitting meditating for improving their lives and deepening their awareness. But you don't have to be seated to meditate. Marital artists, especially T'ai Chi practitioners, consider their art a moving meditation. Runners and other athletes describe meditative experiences and spiritual awakenings while engaged in their sport. As you will be reminded, meditation is not just a mental practice, it is a body-mind experience. If you engage both body and mind, you can turn anything you do into a meditation. If you are new to meditation and having trouble sitting still, try movement meditation to help you get started. Experiment with these wonderful alternatives to the cushion.

Start with the 'Labyrinth' meditation, a wonderful exercise practised worldwide since ancient times. Walking the labyrinth helps you get to the essence of a problem, discover your true nature and balance your body and mind. If you are a runner, 'Runner's way' will help you meditate during your morning run and transform your usual routine. If you are a gardener, you will have a chance to turn 'Weeding' into a fantastic meditative practice for lessening your negative emotions. 'Walking Zen' introduces you to a Zen Buddhist mindful walking practice called *kinhin*.

Have you ever felt that you had entered another plane while dancing? If so 'Dance trance' is for you. If you are adventurous, try 'Whirling dervish' and have a taste of Sufi spinning meditation. The famous mystical poet Rumi invented spinning as a meditative practice for centring and opening your heart to the Divine. If you are already a yoga practitioner, you are probably familiar with 'Sun salutation', one of the most famous and well-loved yoga sequences. Swimming is one of the most meditative sports, so it is a natural for focused meditation. Try 'Swimming to enlightenment' if you want to get the most out of those laps. Want a clean house? Why not use 'Clean sweep' to clear negative thinking while you clean. 'Treadmill' helps you combine your workout with meditation on your breath, to double the benefit of working out.

LABYRINTH

Labyrinth-walking was practised in ancient Crete, Egypt, Peru, India and Ireland. You walk meditatively along a path that cuts back and forth through a series of curves or spirals until you arrive in the centre.

Benefits

- Helps you find your spiritual centre
- Brings more depth to your prayer
- Helps you solve problems

If you check a search engine on the Web, you can locate labyrinths worldwide. Many churches and retreat centres have permanent labyrinths on their property that are open to the public. Walking a labyrinth helps you connect your right and left brain, which encourages creative thought and problem-solving. As you walk the winding path towards the centre of the labyrinth, you may gain more insight into your life or a problem you are trying to resolve.

Meditation

When

Practise labyrinth-walking whenever you want to understand yourself better or get to the heart of any issue.

Preparation

Locate a labyrinth near you. If you can't find one, you can meditate by tracing your finger on a printed labyrinth.

Practice

1 Stand at the entrance of the labyrinth and focus on a problem or concern. For example, you may have a decision to make about a new job.

2 As you enter the labyrinth and begin walking, explore what you think about the problem. As you get deeper into the labyrinth, switch your meditation to what you feel about the problem. What emotions arise?

3 Continue towards the centre asking how this problem affects your material world, your finances or your health. Then ask how this problem affects your spiritual life.

4 When you arrive at the centre, ask your higher power for assistance in solving your problem. Stand silently and see what emerges. Accept it without judgement. If nothing comes to mind, be patient. An answer may come to you some days later.

5 On your walk back out of the labyrinth, meditate on any solution that emerged. If none emerged, concentrate on placing one foot in front of the other. When you reach the exit of the labyrinth, stand for a moment and thank your higher power for his or her help with your problem.

RUNNER'S WAY

If you are a runner, you may have already experienced a meditative state while running. Use this meditation to make your meditation more focused and conscious.

Benefits

- Elevates running to a spiritual activity

- Encourages mindfulness

- Reduces stress and depression

Meditation

When

Meditate whenever you run by yourself.

Preparation

Try to be in the present moment, mindful of everything that is around you.

Practice

1 Begin meditating as you put on your t-shirt, shorts and running shoes. Do this mindfully, focusing on each task.

2 As you begin running, meditate as you would for 'Watching your breath' on pages 50–1 except you are moving instead of sitting down on a cushion or chair.

Researchers have found that running and meditation both have a positive effect on your mood. Runners and meditators experience the elevation of a specific hormone that enhances well-being. If you have a sedentary job, perhaps sitting in front of a computer screen for most of your day, you need to move when you are not at work. If you are a runner, why not combine it with meditation for double the benefit?

3 Now let go of your concentration on your breath, and focus on the act of running. Try not to let thoughts enter your mind; when they do, simply return your focus to your running. Begin to feel your body, mind and soul functioning together as one. Continue to stay in the present moment, very much aware of everything around you.

4 When you finish your run, take off your shoes and socks and stand on the grass. Feel connected to the Earth and grounded in your body. Continue to be mindful of the present moment throughout your day.

WEEDING

If you are a gardener, you understand weeding. Why not make your weeding into a meditative practice? If you don't have a garden, offer to weed for someone else or volunteer with your local parks service.

Benefits

- Elevates gardening to a spiritual activity

- Helps reduce negative emotions

- Promotes positive growth

Visualization has a powerful effect on your mind. If you want to make positive changes in your life, visualization can turbo-charge the process. In this meditation, you use weeds to symbolize any negative habits that you want to drop.

Meditation

When

Try this meditation when doing some gardening.

Preparation

Get out your gardening gloves and knee pads. Collect any tools you might need such as a trowel or gardening fork.

Practice

1 Sit quietly under a tree. Bring to mind any negative habits you may have, such as a tendency to bad temper or procrastinaton. Think of as many as you like. Visualize the weeds in the patch as your negative habits.

2 Get up from under the tree and approach the area you are planning to weed. See that whole area as you or your mind. See the flowers and plants as your positive traits and the weeds as those negative traits that you would like to eliminate.

3 As you begin to weed, try to stay very focused and mindful. When you pull out a weed by its roots, think that you are pulling out your own negative habit by the roots. Continue in this way until all the weeds are removed.

4 Finish by cultivating, feeding and watering the plants and flowers. Think of them as your positive traits that you would like to nurture.

WALKING ZEN

Zen Buddhists practise a wonderful walking meditation called *kinhin*. You do not have to be a Buddhist to enjoy this calming, centring, mindful and moving meditation.

Benefits

- Extends practice of concentration to walking

- Helps integrate your focused mind with movement

- Provides relief during longer sitting meditation sessions

Meditation

When

Try this when you want to slow down and be more precise in your work or relationships.

Preparation

Mark out a route before hand, either in your house or outdoors.

Practice

1 Stand with your back straight and try to remain relaxed. Place your hands together just below your sternum or heart, with your left hand in a soft fist, wrapping your fingers lightly around your thumb. Then place your right hand over your left with your right thumb across the top of your left hand. Keep your elbows slightly extended from your sides.

In traditional Zen, you practise *kinhin* walking meditation in between long sessions of sitting meditation or *zazen*. It relieves any stiffness from sitting and energizes you. But you can practise *kinhin* as a meditation on its own. You can do walking meditation indoors by circling around a room or by walking outdoors in your garden or along a path. If outdoors, it should be where you can be alone.

2 Begin walking slowly along the route you decided on in your preparation, either inside or outside. Begin by taking a half-step with every cycle of breath (inhalation and exhalation). So, it is heel first (half-step) and ball of foot (half-step). Your pace will be extremely slow. As you walk, focus on your breath. Keep your eyes lowered and directed straight ahead. Don't look from side to side.

3 Stop. Now switch to a normal walking pace for a few minutes. Keep focusing on your breath. Breathe naturally. End your meditation when you feel ready to do so.

DANCE TRANCE

You can say your prayers, but you can also dance your prayers.
Dance can help you transcend your ordinary mind and access the
Divine. Try this dancing form of meditation.

Benefits

• Helps you access both
  hemispheres of your brain

• Releases resistance to the
  Divine

• Helps ground your body
  and promote wellness

This is movement as a spiritual practice. It
can be lots of fun and it can bring up a flood
of other emotions. If you end up laughing or
crying, your tendency may be to stop. It is
important to keep dancing no matter what
happens. Dance through any feelings and see
what emerges. This meditation is about
emotional, physical and spiritual release. The
idea is to transcend your usual left-brained
linear thinking and access the wisdom of your
body in movement. Through dance and
letting go of thought, you may have
realizations about reality not normally
available to you in ordinary life.

Meditation

When

If you feel that you are about to explode from stress and unexpressed emotions, try this dancing mediation to help you figure out what is going on.

Preparation

Listen to trance music or other music with a strong rhythm. Choose several CDs that appeal to you.

Practice

1 Find time when you can be alone. Go barefoot or wear shoes you can dance in comfortably. Wear clothes that are very loose and free. Take off your glasses and wristwatch. Now clear the area in which you are going to dance.

2 Put on the music and turn it up as loud as possible. Begin dancing and don't stop for 30 minutes. If you want to keep dancing for longer, do so.

3 While you are dancing try to focus on your dance. Try not to think and carry on dancing until you are exhausted. Try to feel connected to your higher power as you dance. If you feel emotional or feel like crying, don't hold back.

4 When you feel that you have danced as much as you can, end your dance meditation.

WHIRLING DERVISH

Sufis practise whirling or spinning to get in touch with the Divine. Accompany your whirling with trance-like music and see what happens and how it makes you feel.

Benefits

- Encourages surrender to the Divine

- Opens you to ecstatic joy

- Promotes a feeling of being immersed in the grace of God

Jalaluddin Rumi, born in Persia in 1207, is perhaps the most famous Sufi master. He is most well known in Western culture for his exquisitely beautiful devotional poetry. While overcome with grief over the loss of a dear friend, he began practising whirling as a means of communing with God. The purpose of meditation by spinning is to induce a religious trance, so that wherever you turn, you see the face of God. With practise, and by focusing on your hand, it is possible to whirl for long periods of time without getting dizzy.

Meditation

When

Try whirling as a form of meditation when you are open to having an ecstatic connection with the Divine.

Preparation

Practise whirling with your eyes closed. Try rotating your head as you turn. Find instrumental music to accompany your whirling.

Practice

1 Start playing your chosen CD. Stretch your right arm out in front of your body, with the palm of your hand facing your heart. Extend your left arm up towards heaven.

2 Fix your gaze on the hand in front of you and begin turning slowly clockwise. If it feels better to turn counterclockwise, reverse your hand positions. It is said that turning counterclockwise feels more inward and clockwise more outward.

3 If you should start to feel dizzy, simply slow down. Try pivoting on your heel, then the ball of your foot to see what works best for you. Rotate your head while you whirl.

4 To end your whirling meditation, slow down gradually and stop. Stand quietly for a few moments.

SUN SALUTATION

This famous yoga asana, *surya-namaskar*, will get you moving early in the day. Practise this as a meditation first thing in the morning to engender a sense of gratitude and purpose.

Benefits

- Promotes physical, mental and emotional well-being
- Sets your higher intention for the day
- Encourages gratitude and responsibility

Surya-namaskar, or sun salutation, is a 12-part pose that is invigorating and energizing. Try practising this pose meditatively, concentrating on what you would like to accomplish during the course of this day. As you greet the sun, express your thanks for being alive and having the opportunities you have been given.

Meditation

When

Practise sun salutation in the morning.

Preparation

Read through the directions and practise each step before trying it as one sequence.

Practice

1 Stand with your feet hip-width apart, hands by your sides.

2 Inhale, and raise your arms up overhead and gently arch back as far as feels comfortable.

3 As you exhale, bend forward and rest your hands beside your feet.

4 Inhale and step the right leg back while your hands remain on the floor.

5 Exhale and step the left leg back. Now you are in a push-up position with arms fully extended. Hold the position and inhale.

6 Exhale and lower yourself as if coming down from a push-up. Only your hands and feet should touch the floor.

7 Inhale and stretch forward and up, bending at the waist. Use your arms to lift your torso, but only bend back as far as feels comfortable.

8 Exhale, lift and push your hips back and up with your head facing down between your straight legs.

9 Inhale and step your right foot forward.

10 Exhale, bring your left foot forward and pull your head to your knees.

11 Inhale and stand tall while keeping your arms extended over head.

12 Exhale and lower your arms to your sides. Repeat the sequence, stepping back with the left leg first.

SWIMMING TO ENLIGHTMENT

If you are a swimmer, why not turn those laps into meditation? Bring this wonderful visualization into the pool with you and transform your body and your mind at the same time.

Benefits

- Transforms ordinary swimming into spiritual practice

- Provides a powerful meditation for overcoming obstacles

- Helps balance your body and mind

Meditation

When

Try this meditation when swimming laps.

Preparation

Write about what might be holding you back. Are you afraid to express yourself directly? Do you wish you could be more organized? Do you want to practise a spiritual path but find that doubts get in your way?

Practice

1 Select a free lane and begin swimming laps. For the first few minutes simply watch your breath as you swim.

2 Bring to mind the obstacle you want to overcome. See yourself being held back in a situation because of some aspect of your character or personality. For example, if you

Swimming, like running, is another athletic activity that lends itself to meditation. It is a solitary practice, regardless of how many others are in the pool with you. It is inherently rhythmic, relaxing and inspires introspection. Simply try watching your breath while swimming or combining other meditations in this directory with swimming. If you want to remove obstacles in your life, try this visualization.

are afraid to express yourself at work, imagine yourself at the office feeling frustrated and ashamed because you are afraid to speak up to your boss.

3 Then with each stroke, visualize that you are making headway, overcoming your fear. See yourself walking into your boss's office, confidently sharing your brilliant ideas.

4 Swim as many laps as you want, using each stroke as a symbol of your progress in removing your obstacles – be they mental, psychological or spiritual.

CLEAN SWEEP

Sweep the floor when you want a clean house. Transform it into a moving meditation for clearing negative thinking, emotions and states of mind.

Benefits

- Transforms ordinary house-cleaning into spiritual practice
- Provides powerful visualization for clearing negativity
- Strengthens spiritual resolve

Sweeping is one of the more satisfying house-cleaning activities. It is physical and you can see the results immediately. There is something wonderful about cleaning all that dust and dirt out of the way. Vacuum if you must, but this meditation is best done with a good old-fashioned broom.

Meditation

When

When you have to house-clean anyway, you can make good use of your time with this meditation.

Preparation

Think of any past negativity you would like to purify or any mental debris you would like to clear.

Practice

1 Pick up your broom and stand in the area you plan to sweep. It can be inside or outside your house. Kitchen or garage floors work nicely and your path or front step would be fine as well.

2 Examine the floor for dust or dirt. It may be quite noticeable or quite subtle. See that noticeable or subtle dust or dirt as negativity residing in your own mind and heart. Imagine that as you sweep, the negativity will be swept away with the dirt. If you have been unkind to your partner, if you have hurt a friend or if you have been drinking too much lately, see the dirt as these past actions.

3 Start sweeping. Focus only on the dirt, the broom and the floor. As you sweep, see and feel your negativity leaving your mind and heart. You can sweep away your potential to commit negative acts in the future and your doubts and your fears in the present. Get creative and sweep away whatever is bothering you.

4 End your meditation by sweeping the dirt into a bin and throwing it away. See your negativity going with it.

TREADMILL

If you belong to a gym, you probably use a treadmill for aerobic exercise. Instead of entertaining yourself by listening to music or watching television, use the time for meditation.

Benefits

- Doubles the benefit of working out
- Connects your body and mind
- Inspires spirtual practice

There is something about a treadmill that seems a lot like life. It is common to hear someone say they 'feel like they are on a treadmill'. It usually means they feel they are running along going nowhere. But any action can be transformed by your mind and your intention. Use aerobic exercise to doubly improve your cardiovascular health by working with your mind at the same time. This is a good way to keep your workouts from becoming yet another frenetic activity in an already busy life.

Meditation

When

Try this meditation when you want to make your workouts mentally and physically rejuvenating.

Preparation

Go to the gym when it is less busy so that you can stay on the treadmill for as long as you like.

Practice

1 Before you step on the treadmill, stop for a minute and set your intention to meditate. Begin your workout slowly. Work up to a speed at which you can walk or run for 30 minutes. Set the timer. Put a towel over the digital readout so that it will not distract you.

2 Now begin watching your breath. At first count up to ten and then start again. Try not to let thoughts intervene.

When they do, simply return to your breath. When you feel like it, let go of counting and just watch your breath as you would in seated meditation.

3 If emotions arise, just acknowledge them and return to your breath. If you feel the healthy stress of running, note it and return to your breath.

4 End your meditation after 30 minutes. Note any difference that there has been between this workout and your normal one.

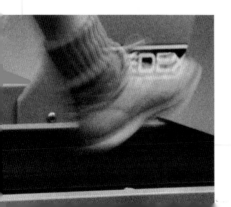

LOVE AND COMPASSION

MEDITATIONS FOR LOVE AND COMPASSION

More than anything else, love and compassion uplift and transform your life. They reduce your anger, hatred and jealousy, while expanding your heart and mind, making life worthwhile. When all is said and done, there is nothing more important than love and compassion.

This section starts with three meditations on an extraordinary Tibetan Buddhist practice called *tonglen*. In this practice you learn to receive, through your in-breath, the suffering of yourself and others, and send, through your out-breath, your love and joy. It is one of the most rewarding and transformative meditations in this book. In 'Repaying kindness' you learn to recognize the boundless kindness of others, and in 'Forgiveness' you let go of past hurt and resentment. Next, you will learn a beautiful Buddhist prayer called the 'Four Immeasurables', and you will learn compassion for animals in a wonderful meditation ritual called 'Free sentient beings'. Love is the answer in 'Love yourself' and 'Unconditional love'. And if you have difficult relationships with your siblings, try 'Brothers and sisters'.

World peace is everyone's wish. 'Peace starts with me' helps you do your part. 'Heart *chakra*' helps you work directly with your heart energy. Try

'Mothers and fathers' for loving and forgiving your parents, and 'Fear and love' if you are simply afraid to love. 'Expand your heart' will help you overcome prejudice. With 'All beings want to be happy' you will focus on love, while in 'All beings want to avoid suffering' you will focus on compassion, and understand how they are linked.

Equanimity is the basis of love and compassion and 'Three boxes' will help you understand why we have trouble treating everyone equally. Affection is simple yet we don't have enough in our lives. Learn to give and receive it with 'Affection'. And the next time you see a homeless person, go home and try the 'Homelessness' meditation. It will help you have compassion for those suffering silently in our cities and towns.

'Interconnectedness' teaches you how everything and everyone is connected, an important point when it comes to love. 'To be of service' helps you know how to best help others. 'Love and attachment' will help you recognize true love and 'Unlimited love' will help you to be more generous with your love. Finally, 'The *Bodhisattva* vow' will introduce you to a Buddhist way of deepening your love and compassion.

TONGLEN FOR YOURSELF

Tonglen is a Tibetan Buddhist practice for developing compassion. In the *tonglen* visualization, you receive, with an open heart, the suffering of others and give selflessly all of your love, joy and well-being to them. It is best to practise *tonglen* for yourself first.

Benefits

- Brings your difficulties and illness into your spiritual path

- Helps you stay present in difficult situations

- Develops compassion for yourself

You practise this meditation by receiving difficulties and suffering through your in-breath and by exhaling joy and love on your out-breath. Accept on your in-breath; let go on your out-breath. You inhale your own conflicting emotions and negative karma and exhale your compassion and love for yourself.

Meditation

When

Practise *tonglen* for yourself when you are having difficulties or problems with chronic self-hatred. You can practise this meditation at any time, anywhere.

Preparation

Acknowledge any difficulties you may be having.

Practice

1 For formal practice, sit in meditation posture on your cushion or chair in a quiet place. Or you can practise whenever and wherever you like.

2 Focus on any difficulties you are currently experiencing. If you are sad and regretful or if you are stressed out about money, bring that problem to your full awareness.

3 Breathe your problems and difficulties into your heart. Visualize your difficulties being dissolved and transformed. Now see them ride out on your out-breath as happiness and joy, luminosity and fearlessness.

4 Practise *tonglen* with the hope of healing your attitude and restoring yourself to wholeness. Continue exhaling and inhaling, riding your breath in this way for as long as you like.

TONGLEN FOR OTHERS

After practising *tonglen* meditation for yourself, this *tonglen* meditation will teach you how to practise it in order to develop feelings of compassion for others.

Benefits

- Helps you to develop compassion for others

- Transforms your relationships

- Develops generosity and non-attachment

After you have experienced compassion for yourself, extend your love and compassion to those who are close to you – your parents, your family, your children and friends. Gradually extend compassion until you are able to feel it for enemies as well as friends. Finally, extend your caring to all beings in the world. Imagine them soothed and healed by your love. It is best to begin with those closest to you.

Meditation

When

Practise *tonglen* for others for those close to you when you become aware that they are suffering.

Preparation

Practise *tonglen* for yourself first, to begin to understand what compassion feels like.

Practice

1 Sit in meditation posture on your cushion or chair or practise spontaneously any time and anywhere you want. Breathe for a few minutes to calm your mind. Then imagine having unlimited love and compassion.

2 Think of someone close to you, who you know is suffering from life problems or illness. Visualize the person in front of you.

3 Breathe in their suffering in the form of black smoke and let it gather in your heart. Be willing to take it on and remove it from them. As it reaches your heart imagine it dissolving all your self-centredness. Now breathe out love, joy and compassion to him or her. Dont hold anything back.

4 When you first start this practise, you may have some difficulty visualizing taking in other peoples' suffering and giving away all your joy and happiness to them. But over time, this will change. You will discover that you have an abundance of positive resources, more than you can imagine. And don't worry – taking in other peoples' problems in this way will not harm you.

5 Continue taking and sending on your breath for as long as you like. End when you are ready.

TONGLEN FOR NEGATIVE ENVIRONMENTS

You can also practise *tonglen* to transform negative environments. Wherever you are, if the atmosphere is angry, tense or oppressive, practise *tonglen* to remove the negativity and provide a safe, compassionate space for yourself and others.

Benefits

- Helps transform negative environments
- Creates positive environments
- Creates compassionate space

Meditation

When

Practise *tonglen* when the atmosphere or environment is oppressive or negative.

Preparation

Try '*Tonglen* for yourself' and '*Tonglen* for others' before trying this meditation.

Practice

1 Stand in the space that feels oppressive or negative. Centre yourself by meditating on your breath for a few minutes. Set a compassionate motivation – you would like to relieve the negativity in this room or space for the benefit of those who will be meeting here. Imagine you feel love and compassion equally for all beings.

You have heard the expression, 'the atmosphere was so tense, you could cut it with a knife'. Negative energy can 'charge' and change a room, even after those responsible for creating it leave. That residual negative energy can affect your well-being and that of others.

2 Breathe in the negativity of the room in the form of a cloud of hot, dark smoke. See it entering your heart where it is transformed into clear, calm, clean, cool air. When you exhale, send it out as peace and joy. Visualize radiant, pure light filling the room, creating a loving, compassionate, soothing environment for everyone who enters.

3 Continue breathing in this way until you have transformed the energy or atmosphere in the room or you are ready to end your meditation. Don't worry if you don't feel a dramatic change. Know that by meditating in this way, you are making the world a more compassionate place for all who live in it.

REPAYING KINDNESS

This is a wonderful meditation for realizing the kindness of others. It will help you develop compassion and reduce any self-centredness that may creep into your thoughts or behaviour.

Benefits

- Reveals how much you owe others
- Develops compassion
- Counteracts self-centredness

It may seem you have accomplished everything in your life by your own efforts. Since you have had to work very hard to get through school, then get a job, find a partner and raise your family, it is easy to think this way. But nothing can be further from the truth. Your efforts have been very important, but you have had enormous help from countless beings along the way. This meditation helps you recognize those countless beings.

Meditation

When

Try this meditation when you are feeling alone and struggling.

Practice

1 Sit on your meditation cushion or chair. Light a candle in memory of all those who have helped you in your life.

2 Recall the list you made in preparation for your mediation. Begin with your mother and father; then go on to siblings, aunts and uncles, grandparents and cousins, all of whom cared for you in some way. Then think of your teachers, your babysitters, clergy, coaches and friends. Think of your first job and the person who hired you. Now consider the farmers who grew the food you ate and the shops that sold the food.

Preparation

Make a list of everyone who took care of you as a child.

Return to your parents who worked hard for you to have a home, clothes, food, schooling and medical care. Think of your doctors and dentists. Your list is merely the tip of the iceberg.

3 Continue to add to your list. Generate a sincere sense of gratitude to every person who helped you in your life. Realize you have been the recipient of so much kindness it will take lifetimes to repay everyone. Vow to pay back all of that kindness by generating love and compassion for them and for all beings.

FORGIVENESS

There is nothing more difficult or more rewarding than forgiveness. You can forgive yourself and others once you have done the emotional work necessary to process your feelings and let go of always having to be 'right'.

Benefits

- Promotes peace
- Encourages compassion
- Reduces rigid and inflexible thinking

This meditation on forgiveness is grounded in the reality that you and others are in a constant state of change. Although it may appear so, you are not the person you were yesterday or even a minute ago, nor is the person who harmed you. Forgiveness helps you shed your pain and anger, and opens your heart once again.

Meditation

When

This meditation helps to heal anger and pain when you are feeling wounded over someone else's actions.

Preparation

It is important to feel everything you may be feeling about the event that caused you harm before you can begin to heal your anger and pain.

Practice

1 Sit on a cushion or chair in your meditation space. If you have an altar, meditate on your chosen higher power. Light a candle and make simple offerings of flowers or fruit. Ask for help in forgiving the person who harmed you.

2 Recall the event in which you felt harmed. If your first emotion is anger, look underneath for hurt. As you think about and feel what happened, try not to vilify the other person. Simply admit how you are feeling.

3 Now think of the other person. See them as a whole person who is more than their actions and who is changing every moment. Understand that they did what they did because they thought it would make them happy and help them avoid suffering. Their motivations are no different from yours.

4 Forgive the person who hurt you. Say this out loud. Wish them to be happy and free of suffering. Open yourself to the possibility of healing your relationship in the present. If that's not possible, simply let go of your anger and pain. See it as a large heavy suitcase that you refuse to carry any longer.

5 Thank your higher power for helping you see the bigger picture.

FOUR IMMEASURABLES

This meditation is a wonderful antidote to the nightly news. You wish that an immeasurable number of beings have immeasurable love, compassion, joy and equanimity.

Benefits

- Promotes love and compassion

- Includes yourself in your intentions

- Encourages spiritual growth

The 'Four immeasurables' is a Tibetan Buddhist meditation. Its purpose is to help you feel more kindness and compassion towards yourself and towards others.

You will need to memorize the following prayer for this meditation

May all beings have happiness
May all beings be free from suffering
May all beings find joy that has never known suffering
May all beings be free from attachment and hatred.

Meditation

When

Meditate on the 'Four immeasurables' on a daily basis.

Preparation

Memorize the short prayer opposite.

Practice

1 Sit on a cushion or chair in your meditation space. Meditate on your breath for five minutes.

2 Recite out loud the first line of the prayer: 'May all beings have happiness'. Feel your intention that all beings have your unconditional love. Include yourself in this wish. Accept them and yourself exactly as they and you are.

3 Move to the second line and say it loud, 'May all beings be free from suffering'. Imagine that you have infinite compassion and wish all beings, including yourself, to be free from suffering of any kind. Bring to mind any form of suffering. It could be someone with cancer or your own suffering from illness or addiction. Feel a great urgency to help them and yourself.

4 Recite the third line: 'May all beings find joy that has never known suffering'. Imagine that all beings have enlightenment, the ultimate spiritual development in Buddhism. Feel the depression of all beings, including yourself, lifting and being eradicated. Imagine they and you are in a blissful, happy, unselfish, enlightened state.

5 Recite the fourth line: 'May all beings be free from attachment and hatred'. Imagine that all beings, including yourself, never distinguish between a friend, enemy or stranger, but regard all beings, regardless of who they are, as worthy of love and compassion. Know this equanimity is the basis for the first three wishes – unconditional, altruistic love, compassion and pure joy.

FREE SENTIENT BEINGS

This practice helps you to generate more compassion for all non-human sentient beings, including animals, birds, insects and fish. In this meditation, you free animals, birds, fish or insects that might otherwise be killed.

Benefits

- Promotes sensitivity to the plight of animals and other beings

- Encourages love and compassion

- Promotes compassionate action

Meditation

When

Try doing this meditation practice as a ritual once a year.

Preparation

Find an animal, an injured bird, a fish or an insect that you can release safely into the wild. Make sure it is in the best interest of the being you are releasing. You can find good subjects in a fisherman's bait shop, such as worms or tiny fish compatible with your local environment.

Practice

1 Take your animal, bird, fish or insects to the place where you will release them.

2 Stand or sit comfortably and focus on your breath for a few minutes to centre yourself.

If you love animals, you will find this meditation very enjoyable. If you don't think about animals very often, this meditation will help you become more sensitive to the reality of those beings that dwell in the 'animal realm'. In Buddhism, the animal realm is comprised of all non-human living beings, not just animals as we normally understand them.

3 Think for a moment of all suffering beings in the animal realm. Visualize the difficulties of their lives on a day-to-day basis. Wish for the small beings you are about to release and all others in the animal realm to have happiness and be free from suffering. With that sincere wish, release it into the wild.

LOVE YOURSELF

Self-hatred is common in our culture. This meditation will help you counteract any feelings of self-hatred, including shame or low self-esteem.

Benefits

- Provides an antidote to self-hatred
- Encourages positive self-regard
- Helps you develop love and compassion for others

Little in our lives teaches self-love. You may be berating, disciplining and punishing yourself into the person you think you 'should' be. You may be spending your life feeling that there is something wrong with you, and trying to fix it. This is a form of self-hatred. It is important to approach any self-improvement exercise, including any meditation in this book, from a place of basic self-acceptance.

240

Meditation

When

Try this meditation when you become aware of self-hatred.

Preparation

Monitor any self-talk for a day and notice how much of what you say to yourself is negative. It may show up as 'I'm a stupid idiot for forgetting that memo', or 'I hate my thighs'.

Practice

1 Sit on a cushion or chair in a quiet place. Visualize your higher power sitting in front of you. It could be Jesus, Buddha, Shakti, Mohammed or just a wise form of your self.

2 Imagine your higher power smiling at you with great love and compassion, accepting you as you are. Understand that he or she does not demand that you 'fix' anything about yourself to deserve his or her love. Know that he or she wants you to accept yourself exactly as you are, and treat yourself with kindness and respect as they already do.

3 Thank your higher power for reminding you to be kind towards yourself. Tell him or her that with their help and encouragement, you will refrain from hating yourself and will encourage yourself to accept yourself exactly as you are. Promise that you will try to live your life with complete self-acceptance and self-love.

UNCONDITIONAL LOVE

Most often our love is conditional – on whether our loved ones behave the way we would like or support us in our endeavours. But a better love is one without conditions – we love them as they are, regardless of what they do.

Benefits

- Elevates ordinary love
- Frees us to love all people
- Promotes spiritual development

Unconditional love sounds good, but is difficult to practise. This meditation will help open your heart and release the conditions you may be placing on your love. If you have problems with co-dependence or trying to control those you love, this meditation will help.

Meditation

When

Practise this meditation if you have control issues in your relationships.

Preparation

Think of those closest to you. Ask yourself if you have put conditions on your love for them. For example, you may feel your love depends on someone loving you back in the way you want. Realize that this is limited conditional love.

Practice

1 Sit on a cushion or chair in your meditation space. Make sure you have privacy. Begin by watching your breath and calming body and mind.

2 Bring to mind your partner or other loved one. List any conditions you have that limit your love for them. For example, you may find you love them on condition that they make a lot of money, buy you flowers for special events or wear certain clothes. Note how these conditions, while seeming practical and rational, constrict your heart. Note how this doesn't sound like love, but more like a demand that your needs be met.

3 Now visualize giving your loved one complete freedom to be and do what they want. Does this frighten you, make you sad or change how you feel about them? Bring to mind the qualities you love about this person. Perhaps you love their energy, their courage and their ability to respond to others.

4 Imagine them not being with you or available to meet your needs and loving them anyway. Feel your heart expand as you accept and love them wholeheartedly, regardless of what they do or don't do for you.

BROTHERS AND SISTERS

All religions encourage you to love your parents, but many do not say as much about siblings. Try this meditation to heal your sibling relationship and encourage more love between you.

Benefits

- Places importance on sibling relationships
- Encourages love and respect
- Heals old wounds

You may take your relationships with your brothers and sisters for granted and disregard how deeply they have affected your life. Old rivalries, conflicts or unresolved hurts may be harming you in your adult relationships. You may need to break the old habits that keep you and your siblings frozen in childhood and create a new vision for your present-day family.

Meditation

When

This is a great meditation to practise before a family holiday event.

Preparation

Find photographs of you and your siblings from childhood.

Practice

1 Sit on your cushion or chair in your meditation space. Place the photos of your siblings on your altar. Light a candle. Meditate on your breath for a few minutes. Now call on your higher power to sit alongside you. Introduce him or her to your siblings.

2 Let any feelings emerge. Ask your higher power to help you heal your relationships, if they need healing. If they don't, ask that your relationships deepen and strengthen over your lifetimes. If you have unproductive ways of relating that

are rooted in your childhood, ask that you be able to shed them and find a new, more mature model.

3 Now recall the positive qualities in each of your brothers and sisters. Ask that you be able to accept and love them exactly as they are.

4 Close your meditation by committing to honour and respect each of your siblings and strengthen the relationships you have with them.

PEACE STARTS WITH ME

One of the best ways to work for peace is to work on generating peace in your own circle – with your loved ones, your friends, your co-workers, your neighbours and other community members.

Benefits

- Promotes peace
- Encourages responsibility
- Promotes better inter-
personal communication.

Peace can only spread through individuals who have peaceful minds. If you want a peaceful mind, start reducing your own hatred and violence through patience and tolerance. If you feel rage over something your spouse did and speak harshly to him or her, or if you scream at your kids and hit them, you are practising hatred and violence. This visualization meditation will help plant the seeds of peace in your own heart so that you can be a source of peace to others.

Meditation

When

If you are appalled at the hatred and violence in the world, look into your own thoughts and actions. Determine to root out any seeds of hatred and violence in your own thoughts and behaviour. In this way you can begin to create world peace.

Preparation

Take a few days to thoroughly review your own life for signs of hatred and violence.

Practice

1 Sit on a cushion or chair in your meditation space. Light a candle or incense to help you become calm and centred.

2 Bring to mind any time you have practised hatred or violence in your own life. Perhaps you thought about or talked about someone in your circle in a hateful way. Maybe you 'lost it' in anger and said things that were hurtful to your partner. Recall any time you have been ruthlessly competitive at work. If you have hit a child or pet in anger, don't

minimize its significance. If you can't recall anything specific, look for more subtle states of mind.

3 Forgive yourself for any hateful or violent actions you have taken. Realize that you can make a great contribution to world peace by bringing peace into your being, then into you own circle of family, friends and co-workers. Commit to monitoring yourself for any feelings of hatred and violence. Vow to create more patience and tolerance in your daily life.

HEART CHAKRA

Your heart *chakra* is considered the love centre of the human energy system in the Hindu and Buddhist worlds. It is one of seven energy centres located along the spine and is found in the centre of your chest.

Benefits

- Encourages unconditional love
- Releases sadness
- Opens your heart

Meditation

When

Try this meditation on your birthday.

Preparation

Try to find a diagram of the *chakras* on the Web or in a book on the *chakras*.

Practice

1 Sit on your meditation cushion or chair. Sit up tall with your spine straight and your chest open.

2 Bring your palms together and press the knuckles of your thumbs into your sternum. You will find a notch between your left and right rib cage at the level of your heart. Bring your focus to your

According to the Hindu and Buddhist traditions, your *chakras* can be blocked through loss, fear, anxiety, sadness, anger or stress. This meditation is for healing your heart *chakra*, which governs love and compassion.

thumbs and try to feel the beating of your heart. Focus on your heartbeat for five minutes.

3 Place your right palm in the centre of your chest and the left hand on top of the right. Close your eyes and feel the energy at the centre of your chest. Feel its warmth. Visualize this energy as an emerald green light. Feel it radiating out from your heart into the rest of your body

and back into your heart. Stay with this visualization for as long as you like.

4 Turn your palms outward and away from your body. Visualize the green light from your heart *chakra* flowing out of your palms and into the universe. Imagine that this light is gathering all the love and compassion in the universe and bringing it back to your heart *chakra*.

MOTHERS AND FATHERS

Whether you have had a wonderful relationship with your parents or you have had a difficult one, this meditation will help you love and appreciate them.

Benefits

- Encourages you to appreciate your parents' care of you

- Helps heal old hurts and misunderstandings

- Helps you have a mature relationship with them

Without your parents' love, you would not have taken form in this life. They brought you into the world, sheltered, fed and clothed you. You may have complaints about their parenting, but you still owe them your heartfelt gratitude for giving you life and the opportunity to grow and develop as a human being.

250

Meditation

When

Try this meditation on your birthday.

Preparation

Find photos that you like of your mother and father.

Practice

1 Sit on a cushion or chair in your meditation space. Place the photos of your mother and father on your altar or on a small table in front of you. Light a candle and burn incense to help you focus and clear your mind. If it is your birthday, let the candle serve to mark the celebration.

2 Meditate on your breath while you gaze on the photos of your parents. Let your parents and you symbolically inhabit your space in a peaceful and loving way.

3 Now bring to mind the image of your parents as two young lovers. See them holding you as an infant. Regardless of mistakes they may have made in parenting, remember that they cared for you when you were helpless and utterly dependent. Generate sincere gratitude for their care and protection. If you were adopted, visualize your mother and father as you would like them to have been.

4 Feel in your heart that your parents did the best job they could in raising you. Visualize letting the parents of your childhood go. See them walking away behind you. Look ahead and see the parents of your adulthood. Visualize getting to know them in a new way now that you are separate and independent.

5 End your meditation by wishing both your parents and yourself joy and happiness.

FEAR AND LOVE

You may want to be in a relationship but are afraid to love. This meditation will help you move past your fears and find the courage to love another person.

Benefits

- Heals old wounds that may be standing in your way

- Helps you take risk in opening to others

- Opens your heart

Old wounds may have caused your heart to close tight. You may be afraid to take a risk to be close to someone out of fear of being hurt or fear of abandonment. Face your fear and heal your wounds with this heart *chakra* meditation.

Meditation

When

Try this meditation when you want to open to a new relationship, but fear is getting in your way.

Preparation

Write three pages about why you are afraid of love.

Practice

1 Sit on a cushion or chair in your meditation space. Breathe deeply for a few minutes to clear your mind and energize your body. Focus on your heart *chakra*, located under your sternum.

2 Visualize emerald green light surrounding you. Breathe in the light and let it fill your body. Visualize this healing light entering your heart. Allow it to cleanse and release any fear you have about being used, rejected, manipulated, abandoned or hurt.

3 Continue breathing in the emerald green light. Let go of any fear you have of being controlled, betrayed, lied to or abused. Add any fears to the list that you want. Visualize all your fears evaporating. See your heart relaxing and expanding.

4 Recall anyone in your past who has hurt you. It could be a family member, a friend or an old lover. Forgive them and wish them well.

5 Visualize yourself as strong and in tune with your needs and instincts. Know that you can make good decisions and choose people who are compatible, kind and worthy of your love. Affirm that you will know when to leave a relationship if you feel it is right to do so.

6 Put both hands over your heart. Allow the beautiful emerald green light to recede and your meditation space return to normal.

EXPAND YOUR HEART

If you have any prejudices towards any group because of their race, religion, gender or class, this meditation will help you eliminate it.

Benefits

- Provides an antidote to prejudice and intolerance

- Promotes equanimity

- Expands your heart to accommodate all living beings

Even if you don't have overt prejudices, you may have hidden or unconscious ones. Your willingness to examine your own possible hidden bias is an important step in healing yourself and the world.

Meditation

When

Practise this meditation if you notice that you are pre-judging a person because of their race, religion, gender or social class.

Preparation

Notice how you may be treating people differently because of their race, religion, gender or social class.

Practice

1 Sit on your cushion or chair in your meditation space. Watch your breath for five minutes to centre yourself.

2 Imagine you are facing an assistant at a checkout counter in a shop. Do you feel superior to that person? Are you making assumptions about their intelligence, family background or abilities?

3 Imagine that you are on a bus or train. A person of a different race from you gets on the bus or train. Notice any body reactions you may have. Are you attracted to or repulsed by them? Are you making assumptions about their intelligence, abilities or morality?

4 Now imagine you see a person on television who is a different religion from you. Do you have respect for their religion or do you feel they are 'wrong' in their beliefs?

5 Imagine you are walking down a busy street filled with men and women walking to work. Do you have negative feelings about either sex that colours your feelings about them as individual human beings?

6 End your meditation by committing to let go of any prejudice or stereotypical thinking you may have uncovered.

ALL BEINGS WANT TO BE HAPPY

All beings – humans, animals, reptiles, fish, birds and insects – want to be happy. This is one thing we all have in common. Meditating on this truth will help you better understand the motivations of others, as well as your own.

Benefits

- Helps you understand the motivations of others

- Sheds light on your own motivations

- Generates love and compassion

When you are angry with someone, you may feel you have absolutely nothing in common. The person's behaviour may seem incomprehensible, and his or her thinking deeply flawed. You couldn't be further apart, yet you are operating from the same motivation. Recognizing this common motivation helps you understand others and heals your relationships.

256

Meditation

When

Try this meditation when you are having trouble understanding another person's point of view.

Preparation

Write about how you want to be happy in your own life.

Practice

1 Sit on your cushion or chair in your meditation space. Practise the 'Nine-round breathing' meditation (see pages 58–9).

2 Bring to mind a person with whom you are having difficulties. Perhaps it is your partner or a person in your church group. It could be a parent, sibling or someone at work.

3 Recall something he or she said or did that you found objectionable. Assign a motivation to him or her for what was said or done. In your anger, you may conclude that the person is selfish, manipulative and calculating. You may find his or her motivations to be harmful to others and even morally questionable.

4 Review what you wrote in your preparation about wanting to be happy. Now think of the person with whom you are having difficulties. Realize, like you, he or she is simply trying to find happiness for themselves. The individual may be deluded in their thinking, and in the grip of fear and anger, but his or her motivation is identical to yours.

5 Let this understanding soften your view of the person. You may still disagree with him or her, but you can understand the person a little better. From this place of understanding, you can begin to heal your relationship.

ALL BEINGS WANT TO AVOID SUFFERING

The one thing all beings have in common is that we all want to avoid pain and suffering. Meditating on this truth will help you to better understand the motivations of others, as well as your own.

Benefits

- Helps you understand the motivations of others

- Sheds light on your own motivations

- Generates love and compassion

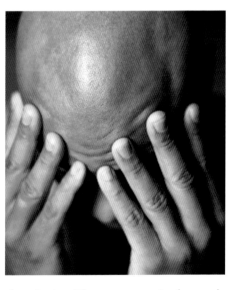

This meditation is very similar to the last one, except this time you recall that every being wants to avoid suffering. This is the second part of universal motivation. The two operate simultaneously, but it is good to meditate on each separately to fully absorb their significance.

Meditation

When

Try this meditation when you are having trouble understanding another person's point of view.

Preparation

First practise 'All beings want to be happy'. Then write down the ways that you are motivated to avoid suffering. For instance, you may eat organic food in order to reduce the risk of cancer.

Practice

1 Sit on your cushion or chair in your meditation space. Practise the 'Nine-round breathing' meditation (see pages 58–9).

2 Bring to mind the same person with whom you were having difficulties in the previous meditation.

3 Recall something he or she said or did that you found objectionable. Assign motivations for the behaviour that made you angry. You may conclude that the person is selfish, manipulative and calculating. You may find his or her motivations to be harmful to others and even morally questionable.

4 Review what you wrote in your preparation about wanting to avoid suffering. Now think of the person with whom you are having difficulties. Realize, like you, that he or she is simply trying to avoid suffering. He or she may fear loss of money or love and the suffering that ensues. Understand that his or her motivation for their actions is identical to yours.

5 Let this understanding soften your view of the person. You may still disagree with him or her, but you can understand the person a little better. From this place of understanding, you can begin to heal your relationship.

THREE BOXES

Equanimity is such an important topic that we have included another meditation on the issue. Combine this meditation with the previous two meditations and discover why you mentally put people in three different boxes.

Benefits

- Helps you understand why you put people in categories
- Reveals the underlying problem of self-centredness
- Helps you practise love and compassion

Equanimity is the basis for love and compassion. It regards everyone as equally deserving of your love and compassion. Without it, you will find yourself preoccupied with sorting people into three boxes – those whom you find attractive, those you dislike and those to whom you are indifferent. This restriction of your love and compassion to those on your 'approved list' diminishes your freedom and joy.

Meditation

When

This is a wonderful meditation to practise on a daily basis.

Preparation

Think of someone whom you find very attractive , someone you find repulsive and someone you have no feelings for, one way or the other.

Practice

1 Prepare yourself to meditate in your meditation space. Begin by watching your breath for a few minutes in order to calm and clear your mind.

2 Begin by thinking of someone whom you find very attractive. Are you seeing him or her clearly? Perhaps you are putting the person on a pedestal. Would you still like the person as much if they were not as beautiful, clever or funny as they are?

3 Next think of a person you find repulsive. Go though a similar exercise. Are you painting a full picture of the person, or making him or her into a two-dimensional caricature? Is any love or care for that person dependent on whether he or she is attractive to you?

4 Finally think of a stranger about whom you have no feelings. Do you feel neutral towards this person because you haven't determined if he or she is useful to you or not? In this way discover the self-centredness inherent in putting people into 'three boxes'.

5 Visualize all three people standing in front of you. Realize all three want to be happy and want to avoid suffering. Imagine feeling love and compassion for all three. Notice if this feels better than sorting them into good, bad and indifferent.

AFFECTION

Visualizing giving and receiving affection can help you to become much more affectionate in all aspects of your daily life. The world needs your tenderness.

Benefits

- Helps you to give and receive affection

- Promotes love and compassion

- Makes your life more enjoyable and fulfilling

If you were wounded as child, you may have trouble giving or receiving a simple hug. You may even find it difficult to be verbally affectionate. Your inhibitions may get in your way.

Meditation

When

Practise this meditation when you are ready to have more affection in your life.

Preparation

Write about your difficulties in giving and receiving affection. Do they stem from your childhood? Was affection not expressed in your family?

Practice

1 Sit on a cushion or chair in your meditation space or find a quiet, private place outdoors.

2 Visualize receiving a hug from a person close to you. Does this feel good and pleasurable to you? If not, breathe deeply and relax your body. Breathe in receptivity and relaxation, breathe out any fear or anxiety you may have over receiving affection, Now try the visualization again. Repeat it until you feel fairly comfortable receiving physical affection.

3 Mentally choose a friend you care about but normally refrain from touching. Imagine expressing your caring with an affectionate hug. Feel any emotions that emerge when you image doing this. If you feel fear or anxiety, or imagine the person rejecting you, breathe deeply for a few minutes, breathing in self-acceptance and breathing out fear of rejection or any other discomfort. Try the visualization again, repeating the process until you feel relaxed and happy hugging and being hugged.

4 End your meditation by giving yourself permission to experiment with giving and receiving affection in your daily life.

HOMELESSNESS

It is easy to forget the homeless, perhaps because you don't want to see them or really know about them. Perhaps they bring up unconscious fears that one day you might be in their place. This meditation will help you to recognize them and develop compassion for them.

Benefits

- Helps you cope with a terrible social problem
- Encourages you to see homeless people as individuals
- Promotes compassion

The homeless are legion. They live in the most prosperous Western countries and in the most impoverished Third World countries. You may feel judgemental about them or feel pity. Neither view is compassionate.

Meditation

When

Meditate on the homeless when you want to develop more compassion.

Preparation

Look at a homeless person directly when you encounter him or her and acknowledge them in some way.

Practice

1 Prepare to meditate in your meditation space. Watch your breath for five minutes in order to calm and centre your mind.

2 Visualize a homeless person you may have seen recently on the street. Recall any negative feelings that arose when you saw him or her. Did you fault the person for their situation? Do you resent his or her presence, dirty clothing or smell? Were you afraid of the person? Did you feel pity?

3 Imagine being that person. Visualize that you once had a job and lived from one payday to the next, but lost your job and had no savings or relatives to help you. You began to drink from the stress. You began to lose your sense of reality. You had no choice but to live on the streets. You wash in public washrooms. You eat leftovers out of bins. You feel shame when people look away. You don't know how this happened to you so quickly. You are overwhelmed and have no hope.

4 See this homeless person as a human being who is suffering. Feel for their suffering. If you want to act on your compassion, volunteer at a homeless shelter or for an organization working to end homelessness. If not, when you next see a homeless person, acknowledge them and view them as an individual who is deserving of your love and compassion.

INTERCONNECTEDNESS

You are connected to everything and everyone else. This meditation on this important fact will help you counteract feelings of alienation, loneliness or meaninglessness, and increase your sense of loving connection to all beings.

Benefits

• Provides an antidote to the feeling that you are separate

• Helps you feel your life has meaning

• Promotes love and compassion

Interconnectedness is not just a spiritual idea. Quantum physics finds you are intimately connected to all reality. In fact, physicists can only observe the particles from which you are made through their interactions with other systems. You may feel alone and separate, but rest assured, you aren't.

Meditation

When

Try this meditation if you are feeling alone, overwhelmed and alienated.

Preparation

Buy an apple at the market.

Practice

1 Sit on a cushion or chair in your meditation space. Bring your apple with you. Watch your breath for a few minutes to calm and settle your mind.

2 Place the apple on your altar or on a small table in front of you. Now visualize the seed from which the apple came. Visualize a farmer planting the seed, carefully fertilizing the ground. Clouds come and go and rain moistens the earth. For years the farmer tends the tree, which is also home to birds and insects, until one day it bears fruit. He hires farm hands to pick the fruit. They pack your apple in a crate with others. The farmer drives your apple to a wholesale market. The wholesaler buys your apple and sells it to your shop. Another driver delivers it to the shop.

A shop assistant arranges it for display. You arrive and pick that apple to use for your meditation.

3 Visualize the apple tree and all the people and equipment involved in bringing this one apple to you. You can extend this meditation by tracing every aspect of the process, including the people who built the vehicle that delivered your apple. At every given moment you are connected to an infinite number of beings. You can't exist without them. You are enmeshed in a cosmic web of creation.

4 End your meditation by eating the apple. Feel your connection to everyone who made it possible.

TO BE OF SERVICE

Our lives have a greater destiny than just our own personal comfort and accomplishment. This meditation will help you expand the meaning of your life to one of service to others as well as yourself.

Benefits

- Expands your motivation for living
- Gives your life a deeper meaning
- Promotes love and compassion for others

You may want to know how you can be of service to your family, your church, your community, your country and the world. Love and service begin at home. Learn to serve those in your immediate circle unselfishly. Try to make your relationships with friends and family sweeter and less demanding.

Meditation

When

Practise this meditation when you want to be of help to others.

Preparation

Think about how you could better serve your family and friends.

Practice

1 Go for a long walk. Begin by watching your breath for a few blocks.

2 Bring to mind your family members and friends. Ask yourself how you could be of service to each of them. Ask yourself how you might genuinely help. Consider each person individually. Ask yourself what you could do to help make their lives easier. It could be something very small. For example, you may decide you could babysit for your sister once a month so that she and her husband could afford to go out for dinner and a movie. You may decide to be more available to your mother who needs someone to talk to since your father died.

3 Now bring to mind your own needs. How can you extend yourself to others and still take care of yourself? Feel yourself shifting your focus to others in a way that is balanced and realistic, in line with what you are capable of. Notice if considering how to meet the needs of others lifts your spirits.

4 End your meditation as you end your walk.

LOVE AND ATTACHMENT

As you have learned in the 'Unconditional love' meditation on pages 242–3, true love doesn't place any conditions on the other person or require them to do anything to earn your love. This meditation explores the same theme in a slightly different way.

Benefits

- Illuminates the difference between love and attachment
- Promotes true love
- Improves your relationships

Meditation

When

This is a good meditation for when you are falling in love.

Preparation

Write about the new person in your life, noting the reasons why you feel you love him or her.

Practice

1 Sit on your cushion or chair in your meditation space. Breathe deeply for several minutes. Now stretch out on the floor in a comfortable position.

2 Imagine you are lying on the grass in a park. Suddenly a beautiful bird lands next to you. It is exquisite. You have never seen such a bird before. Your heart fills with joy as you watch it perched close by, eyeing your with curiosity. You know that it is enjoying being with you too. It stays next to you for the longest time. You feel very

In this meditation you distinguish genuine care from unrealistic projection. It is common to confuse sexual attraction and dependency for love. It is also common to fantasize about a person, to project inflated qualities on to them and mistake this for love. In this case, the person you love doesn't really exist and you find you are attached to an illusion.

connected to the bird. Suddenly, a breeze stirs and the bird disappears into the trees. You are grateful that you had the chance to encounter such a beautiful being and you are happy to know that it exists. You are thankful for the time you spent together.

3 This is the experience of love without attachment. Try to keep this in mind as you begin your new relationship.

UNLIMITED LOVE

This meditation is a good companion to 'Unconditional love'. Not only can love be without conditions, it can be unlimited and embrace everyone, not just the special people in your life.

Benefits

- Extends your ability to love
- Counteracts the idea that love is limited
- Promotes spiritual development

You may conclude that there is only so much love you can give. When you reach the end of your supply, that's it. Therefore, you may find yourself rationing your love, making sure you conserve it and extending it only to those most important to you – your partner, family and best friends. This is a false assumption, since the nature of love is that it is boundless and unlimited.

Meditation

When

Try this meditation when you feel you only have so much love to go around.

Preparation

Think of ten important people and why you love them.

Practice

1 Sit on a cushion or chair in your meditation space. On your alter place an image of a being who, in your mind, embodies unlimited love. It could be God, Christ, Buddha, Quan Yin, Mary, your teacher or anyone you choose. Spend a few minutes looking at the image and contemplating how the love of this deity or teacher feels to you.

2 Imagine extending that unlimited love to everyone with whom you come in contact. Visualize your heart as boundless, feel your love as a bottomless spring that will flow forever. Visualize your love covering the whole planet and everyone in it. All beings are worthy of your love regardless of who they are. Feel your love radiating from your heart in an endless stream. You are fearless, compassionate and tireless in your ability to give love.

3 Now extend your unlimited love to yourself, creating a full circle. End your meditation by placing both hands over your heart and thanking the deity on your altar for their love and inspiration.

THE BODHISATTVA VOW

In Mahayana Buddhism, a *Bodhisattva* is one who has already attained enlightenment but who postpones his or her entrance into nirvana because of profound compassion for others. This meditation introduces you to the vow.

Benefits

- Introduces you to the *Bodhisattva* vow

- Promotes a high motivation for living

- Helps develop compassion for yourself and others

The core of the Mahayana Buddhist path is the *Bodhisattva* vow. In taking the vow, you commit to achieving enlightenment, so as to free all beings from suffering. The emphasis is on compassion and service. You vow to help others while awakening yourself, through the practice of the Six Perfections or Six Virtues, called *Paramitas*. These Six Perfections are: generosity; morality; patience; enthusiasm; meditation and wisdom. You don't have to be a Buddhist or take the vow to meditate on the Six Perfections.

Meditation

When

Practise this meditation if you want these virtues to take hold in your life.

Preparation

Memorize the Six Perfections.

Practice

1 Sit on a cushion or chair in a quiet place. Meditate on your breath for five minutes to calm your mind and prepare to meditate on the Perfections.

2 Think of ways you can be generous with your material possessions, such as giving some money to charities. Work hard to make life safer for people and be generous about sharing your spiritual knowledge.

3 Contemplate morality and how you can better avoid unwholesome actions, live an ethical life and work for the benefit of others.

4 Think about patience and how to tolerate injury and insult without getting angry, how to bear hardship courageously and be patient as you try to develop spiritually.

5 Consider how to develop enthusiasm for your spiritual path, sustain your interest in it and refrain from giving up on yourself.

6 Contemplate meditation and how to control your mind, develop positive qualities through your practice, and develop a peaceful and tranquil mind.

7 Think about wisdom and how to understand the true nature of reality. Understand that everything you do has consequences and everything is interdependent; know what can really help others.

PROBLEM-SOLVING

MEDITATIONS FOR PROBLEM-SOLVING

Meditation is a powerful tool for solving problems. It helps you focus on what is bothering you in a way that ordinary thinking doesn't. When you feel life is getting the best of you, turn to meditation to calm your anxiety. Then continue meditating to face your problems directly and discover creative and effective ways to solve them.

Many people have remarked that if it hadn't been for a particular disaster, they would not have met their true love. Or if they hadn't become seriously ill, they would never have learned to appreciate life fully. This section begins with 'Crisis equals opportunity', a great meditation for finding the hidden gold in the ashes of what seems devastating.

If you are controlling, you are not alone. If you have problems over-managing yourself, others or your environment, try 'You can let go now' to help you understand how fear may be driving you. At times, you may have problems that challenge you morally and ethically. 'High road' helps you stay true to your values in difficult situations, especially when doing the right thing may have some negative consequences for your life. Try 'Walking solution' to help you bring moving meditation to bear on what is bothering you. If you are stressed-out by money – whether it is having it, not having it or wanting it – then try 'Make peace with money'. And if you are in debt, try 'Get out of debt' to help you discipline your spending.

Workaholism used to be considered a problem, now it is expected that you work long hours to get ahead. 'Workaholism' will help you question why you are working so much and help you achieve more balance in your life. 'Facing the mirror' will help you acknowledge your problems, whatever they may be. 'Asking for help' will assist you in getting the help you need.

Seeing the world darkly can be a problem. 'Negative thinking' will help you overcome your self-defeating thoughts. The last meditation in this section, 'Accountability' will empower you to take full responsibility for your life.

CRISIS EQUALS OPPORTUNITY

When a crisis occurs, you can choose to see it as a disaster or you can view it as an opportunity. This meditation will help you focus more positively on the opportunity.

Benefits

- Helps you develop a positive perspective
- Promotes flexibility and creativity
- Reduces stress during a crisis

A crisis can range from stressful to devastating. Perhaps on Friday afternoon you were unexpectedly handed your notice and asked to clear your desk and leave by closing time. Or worse, your home burnt to the ground. Your first response may be to dwell on the disaster, but after the shock passes you can choose to take a different view.

Meditation

When

This meditation will help you in a crisis.

Preparation

Write three pages about what has happened to you. Bring your paper to your meditation session.

Practice

1 Sit on a cushion or chair in your meditation space. Light a candle and if you have an altar, make offerings of flowers and incense to your higher power. Meditate by watching your breath for ten minutes. When you feel calmer move on to the next step.

2 Tell your higher power what has happened to you. If you feel like crying don't hold back.

3 Now ask your higher power to help you see anything positive that can come out of this crisis. Sit quietly and pray for an expanded vision to help you through this difficult time. Pray that your heart and mind be opened to see the opportunity in this crisis.

4 Now write about what opportunities might present themselves in the midst of this disaster. Perhaps you will learn something new, find a better job or make an entirely fresh start in life. If you have lost all your possessions, focus on the freedom rather than the loss. Even if it seems difficult and you don't really believe what you are writing, write anyway. This will sow the seed for you to genuinely feel the opportunity.

5 Close your meditation by thanking your higher power for helping you through this time.

YOU CAN LET GO NOW

Do you have control issues? Has anyone told you that you are controlling? This meditation will help you learn to let go.

Benefits

- Makes life more pleasant for you and others

- Helps you understand that everything changes

- Helps you learn to let go of wanting to control everything

If you are a controlling person, it is important to get beyond your symptoms – your need to control the actions of your loved ones or to have the magazines on the coffee table just so – and ask yourself what you are afraid of. Fear usually motivates the desire to control others or your physical space.

Meditation

When

If you have recieved many complaints about your controlling behaviour, you might want to try this meditation.

Preparation

Write about three occasions on which you can remember feeling anxiety and wanting to control someone else's behaviour, even if it seemed justified to you at the time.

Practice

1 Sit on a cushion or chair in your meditation space. Watch your breath for five minutes.

2 Choose one of the events you listed. Try to recall it in detail. Feel what you were feeling at the time. Perhaps your partner moved a chair and didn't move it back to where you had placed it when he or she left the room. Was your first feeling one of anger?

3 Ask yourself why it is so important to have things the way you want them, especially since you are sharing your life with another person. If you weren't feeling anger, would you feel fear? Are

you afraid something may happen unexpectedly and you will feel powerless, alone, abandoned? Are you trying to ward off unexpected and hurtful things happening by trying to control your environment, the people around you and the future? Explore the fear behind your need to control.

4 Commit to letting go a little at a time on a daily basis by looking for the fear behind the need for you to control. Relax your grip on things and notice that usually nothing terrible happens. Be kind and patient with yourself in this process.

HIGH ROAD

If you are facing a difficult decision, where 'doing the right thing' may have negative consequences for you, it may be hard to follow your moral and ethical principles. This meditation will help you take the 'high road' if that is what you choose to do.

Benefits

- Helps you sort out your moral and ethical views

- Supports you in making a decision, whatever it is

- Encourages you to espouse values based on compassion

Meditation

When

Try this meditation to help you live according to your values.

Preparation

Write about the values you hold dear in your journal.

Practice

1 Sit on a cushion or chair and meditate by watching your breath for five minutes.

2 Bring to mind the situation that is troubling you. If there were no negative consequences, what would you do? What action would feel most congruent with your values? Visualize yourself talking to whomever you need to and taking any action you feel appropriate.

3 Visualize the same situation, but this time bring to mind any negative consequences that may

Has a friend confessed to your that they are stealing from the warehouse at work and selling the material on the side? Do you feel you can no longer work for your company because the managers are knowingly flouting environmental laws, yet you desperately need your job? These are typical situations that present themselves to countless individuals on a daily basis. Meditation can help you sort out what to do.

come your way if you do what you feel is right. Imagine how you will feel if you lost your job or lost your friend? Would you feel more comfortable if you acted in line with how you would like to live your life? Would acting on your principles help some and harm others?

4 Sometimes there are no black or white answers, but spending time quietly trying out ethical decisions is the best way to come to know what is best. Ask your higher power to help you make the most compassionate decision for yourself and any one else involved.

WALKING SOLUTION

Difficult problems sometimes benefit from you taking a good long walk to help sort things out in your mind. This meditation will help you sort out your problems while walking.

Benefits

- Promotes movement to help solve problems

- Helps you sort out how you feel

- Helps you organize the issues

Physical movement is energizing. Walking helps move stagnant energy, promotes better circulation, loosens stiff joints and encourages creative thinking. If you have a problem to sort out, try taking a long walk to focus your mind and expand your options.

Meditation

When

If you have been meditating on a problem and no solution arises, try this walking meditation.

Preparation

Dress appropriately and wear comfortable shoes. Bring water if you think you will need it. Decide on a route that will take about an hour to complete.

Practice

1 Begin your walk by focusing on your breath for about five minutes to calm your mind and settle into your walk.

2 Bring to mind the problem that you can't seem to solve. Visualize that each step you take is bringing you closer to a solution. Then focus on your dilemma. For example, if you are not sure whether you should go back to college, imagine for a five- or ten-minute stretch that you have made the decision to go back to school. See how that feels to your body and mind.

3 For the next five or ten minutes, switch to making the decision not to return to college. Notice how that feels to your body and mind.

4 Now for the rest of your walk, invite an unknown third solution to arise. For example, another solution, besides going or not going to college, may be getting on-the-job training or an apprenticeship. Open yourself to a creative surprise.

MAKE PEACE WITH MONEY

Money – making it, having it, wanting it – is central to most people's lives and a source of great anxiety for many. This meditation helps you make peace with money.

Benefits

- Helps put money in perspective
- Reduces anxiety about money
- Promotes a less materialistic view of life

Money has become the main medium of exchange between people in our cultures. Money determines the value of our time, the value of our possessions and the value of our work. Collectively, as a culture, we have bought into this tendency to measure every aspect of life in money. But there is more to our interactions and in our being than money. Meditation can help free you from this limited and materialistic view of life, and help you make peace with money.

Meditation

When

Try this meditation if you are obsessed with thinking about money.

Preparation

Write about what money means to you and what role it plays in your life.

Practice

1 Sit on a cushion or chair in your meditation space. Make sure your space is private and quiet. Breathe deeply for a few minutes to clear your mind and relax your body.

2 Review what you wrote down in preparation and put it aside. Explore how you feel when you have money. Do you feel more real or substantial? Do you feel you exist more solidly than when you don't have money?

3 Now imagine how you feel when you are broke. Do you feel diminished, deflated and less valuable as a person? Notice you don't become more solid or less substantial when you have or don't have money. Contemplate how money functions as an idea, causing you to feel more or less valuable.

4 Contemplate ten things that are not measured in monetary terms. Your list might include the loving gaze of your partner, a wonderful conversation with a friend, the laughter of your child or the playfulness of your pet.

5 End your meditation by affirming that you are valuable with or without money. Commit to meditating on the meaning of money to help you counteract the cultural message of materialism. Seek out and value those precious experiences money can't buy.

GET OUT OF DEBT

Credit-card debt is on the rise. The habit of living beyond your means may be dragging you down mentally, physically and spiritually. This meditation will help you to find the courage to get yourself out of debt.

Benefits

- Helps you admit that you are in debt

- Supports you in eliminating debt

- Promotes awareness of negative effects of debt

Because credit is easy to obtain, it is easy to use. When you want something, your impulse is to have it now. Your credit-card balance may be increasing every month, you vow to start paying it off, but first you buy just one more thing. And so it goes. This meditation will help you face your debt and do something about reducing it.

Meditation

When

If you have a problem with credit-card debt, practise this meditation on a weekly basis until you are out of debt.

Preparation

Gather your credit-card statements and any other records of debt for your car, house or whatever.

Practice

1 Sit on a cushion or chair in your meditation space. Light a candle to help you focus. Place it on your altar if you have one.

2 Gather your records together and add up how much you are in debt. Say the amount out loud: 'I am [however much] in debt'. Let that fact resonate in your consciousness. How do you feel saying that fact out loud? If you feel numb or if you feel fear, anxiety or shame, note it. How does your body feel when you say the amount out loud? Do you experience a feeling of tension or is your breathing constricted?

3 After admitting to yourself the extent of your debt, generate a sense of compassion for yourself and your difficulties in controlling your spending. From this place of compassion commit to getting out of debt, no matter how long it takes. Ask your higher power to help you control your spending and give you the courage to seek professional help if you need it.

4 End your meditation by placing your statements and credit cards on your altar. Make a promise to your higher power that you will stop spending on credit and will reduce the amount you owe every month by paying off some of the balance.

WORKAHOLISM

What used to be called 'workaholism' is fast becoming the norm for white collar workers. Long hours and taking work home is expected if you want to compete in the corporate world. This meditation helps you to find a better alternative.

Benefits

- Challenges the prevailing work ethic
- Promotes a balanced life
- Helps you stop using work to avoid intimacy

If you are a professional you may be earning an impressive salary. But if you look closer, you may be working 80 hours a week, eating out every night because you are too exhausted to cook and getting your clothes dry-cleaned because you have no time to run the washing machine. You may be expected to spend your time entertaining business contacts and have to travel at the drop of a hat. What is wrong with this picture?

Meditation

When

Try this meditation if you are questioning your fast-paced lifestyle.

Preparation

Write down your typical schedule for a week.

Practice

1 Sit on a cushion or chair in your meditation space. Meditate by watching your breath for five minutes.

2 Look over your schedule. How much time did you spend with your loved ones or friends? Did you get eight hours' sleep a night? When did you relax and play during the week? Did you eat well and exercise? Did you tend to your spiritual life? Are you using your hectic schedule to avoid intimacy? How much money are you really making an hour?

3 Now contemplate your long-term goals? What do you want to achieve? When you are on your deathbed, how do want to have spent your life?

4 Think about the qualities you would like to manifest in your life. Do you want warmth, love, fun, play, spiritual development and time in nature? How is your current life helping you have the quality of life you want?

5 End your meditation by affirming what is most important to you and committing to creating a more balanced life.

FACING THE MIRROR

Everyone has difficulties and problems that persist over time. You are not alone in this. It is time to face your problems directly, with courage and honesty.

Benefits

- Helps you get beyond denial

- Encourages you to face your problems

- Promotes honesty and self-acceptance

This is a simple meditation for overcoming denial. Admitting you have a problem can be difficult. You may feel embarrassed or ashamed, so you simply avoid thinking about it, hoping it will magically resolve itself. Perhaps you have a physical symptom you are afraid to have checked out for fear that it might be cancer. Or you are addicted to shopping and beginning to feel out of control. Or you know you are beyond overweight and, according to the charts, are now obese. It is only human to have problems. What is important is that you face them.

Meditation

When

Try this meditation when you feel you are avoiding your problems.

Preparation

Locate a large mirror and stand up straight in front of it.

Practice

1 Find a time when you can be alone. Stand in front of your bathroom mirror or a full-length mirror.

2 Look at your reflection. Speaking out loud, tell yourself three things you like about yourself. It could be that you are a good listener, a very intelligent person or a great cook. Love the person looking back at you. Tell yourself you know you are struggling, but it is important to admit to the problem that has been dragging you down.

3 Out loud, in a clear voice, tell yourself the problem you have been avoiding. For example, you might say 'I am overweight and I need to lose it for my health and well-being'. Repeat your statement three times.

4 Now commit to taking a step to resolve your problem within the next 24 hours. Say out loud what you plan to do. Repeat it three times.

5 Close your meditation by congratulating yourself for your courage and honesty.

ASKING FOR HELP

If you have a problem, you may find it difficult to ask for help.
You may feel you would rather die than expose your problem to
anyone. This meditation helps you overcome shame to get the
help you need.

Benefits

• Helps you get the
  assistance you need

• Reduces shame

• Gives support and
  encouragement

There are more resources for getting help with psychological, spiritual, health
and financial problems than ever before. And more people are making use of
them. For example, the stigma once attached to seeing a psychotherapist has all
but disappeared. But for a variety of reasons – such as pride, denial and fear –
you may find it difficult to get the help you need.

Meditation

When

If you are having difficulties that you can't resolve on your own, yet you can't seem to ask for help, this meditation is for you.

Preparation

Admit that you need help in solving your problems.

Practice

1 Sit on a cushion or chair in your meditation space. Breathe deeply for a few minutes. Visualize your higher power in front of you. If you don't believe in a higher power, imagine the wisdom aspect of yourself seated before you.

2 Talk to your higher power about the difficulties you are having. If you are struggling with an addiction, tell him or her about it. If you need help to deal with your anger, talk about that. Whatever it is, feel free to tell him or her everything. Visualize your higher power listening to you compassionately and without judgement.

3 Tell your higher power why you have difficulty asking for help. Admit that you need help to overcome your problems and ask for their help in making that phone call or getting that appointment. Imagine him or her being very happy that you have finally let go, admitted your problem and have the wisdom to know that you can't deal with it on your own. Imagine your higher power promising to be with you all the way.

4 End your meditation by committing yourself and your higher power to getting help. Realize that this is a sign of your courage and intelligence.

NEGATIVE THINKING

Negative thinking is one of the most pervasive and universal problems of humankind. If you are a negative thinker, you may not realize the power this habit has over your life.

Benefits

- Exposes your negative thinking habit
- Examines the reasons for negative thinking
- Promotes a more positive view of life

Meditation

When

This meditation is unusual in that you practise it over one full day.

Preparation

Think about the ways in which you are habitually negative in your thoughts or speech.

Practice

1 For one full day, refrain from saying or thinking anything negative. Note when you had the urge to make negative or sarcastic comment or you had negative thoughts about someone or something. As you witness your negative thoughts arise, you will be amazed at the level of negativity in your mind.

How you think determines your reality. If your first inclination is to see the world darkly, you are going to live in a dark world. If your habit is to zoom in on what is wrong with a person, an idea or a thing, the world is not going to be a satisfying place for you. You may think you are simply being realistic, intelligent or discriminating, but you are actually stuck with a warped view of the world. Negative thinking is bad for your health, your relationships and your spiritual life.

2 Be gentle with yourself and simply note the negativity. Don't punish yourself for it. Have a few laughs at how negative your mind can be. Use this meditation to begin to be more positive and supportive in your thoughts and words.

ACCOUNTABILITY

It is easy to blame others for your problems. The habit of assigning blame for your own actions – on others, the weather, the economy or anything else – is dishonest and disempowering.

Benefits

- Helps you be accountable for your actions
- Encourages honesty
- Cuts down on the blame habit

If you are playing the blame game, you are only hurting yourself. Perhaps you are afraid to look at your own behaviour, afraid of judgement or failure. You look anywhere but at yourself when things don't go well. But when you don't feel accountable for your actions, you deprive yourself of the opportunity to learn and grow.

Meditation

When

Try this meditation when you find
yourself in a blaming mode.

Preparation

Recall a recent event where you blamed
others for your difficulties.

Practice

1 Sit on a cushion or chair in your
meditation space. Meditate by
watching your breath for five minutes.

2 Think of a situation or project where
things went wrong, not because of
something you did, but because of
someone's actions. For example, you
may have finished an important proposal
with a deadline for the next day, given it
to an assistant to send overnight, but the
assistant failed to do the job. When your
boss is furious, you in turn blame your
assistant. How do you feel when you
blame your assistant?

3 Now take the viewpoint that you
were accountable for the proposal
being written and delivered on time.
How does this feel? Do you feel more
empowered? When you feel fully
accountable, you can learn from your
mistakes. Perhaps next time you will get
the proposal done early and check to see
that it was sent a day ahead.

4 Think of a similar situation in which
you blamed someone else for your
failure. Reconsider that situation and this
time take full responsibility. What did you
learn? How were you empowered by
being accountable?

MANIFESTING YOUR DREAMS

MEDITATIONS FOR MANIFESTING YOUR DREAMS

Through focused attention and visualization, you can engage your heart and mind in creating the life you want. By meditating on what you want to manifest, you concentrate your energy and support your efforts. Through meditation you engage your powerful subconscious mind in manifesting what you want in life. You also sort out your motivation and reasons for wanting your dreams to come true. In this way you can choose to make sure that what you want not only benefits you but benefits all. The first meditation, 'For the highest good', dwells on this aspect.

So often our childhood dreams are put aside when we become adults. The meditation 'Buried treasure' helps you unearth your own lost dreams. If you are not happy with your work, 'Soul work' will help you find the work that feeds your soul. Where you live can be as important to your happiness as what you do. 'Spirit of place' helps you explore where you will flourish.

We all want that special person in our lives who will be our soul-mate. This person is often a fellow traveller on a spiritual journey, a person who we know so well and have such a deep connection with that we feel we've known him or her for lifetimes. 'Soul-mate' will help you find that person. Your house is an extension of you and a home for your soul. 'Spirit house' helps you to make your living space sacred.

If you want to manifest your dreams, sometimes you have to take a leap. 'Make the leap' will help you find the courage to do so. If you are a procrastinator, your dreams are probably stuck on hold. 'Procrastination' helps you meditate yourself into action. You make many decisions every day. Why not let your higher self make them with 'Spiritual decision-making'.

If you are a visual person, try making a 'Dream map' where you create a visual picture of the dreams you would like to make a reality. 'Take the next step' helps you to recognize and perform the correct action to manifest your dream. 'Follow your bliss' asks you to let joy guide your every decision. Before you can manifest your dreams, you may need to let go of obstacles. 'Let go of your past' will help you let go of old emotional baggage standing in the way of you and your dreams. Finally, if you are an armchair traveller, transform yourself into a real one with 'Traveller'.

FOR THE HIGHEST GOOD

If you have a dream – to start a business, build a house, write a book – manifest your dream, not just for yourself, but for the highest good of all.

Benefits

- Reduces selfishness

- Connects you with all other beings

- Encourages wisdom

Meditation

When

Try this meditation if you want to start a project or manifest a dream.

Preparation

Write about what you would like to manifest. It could be a relationship, a business, a home – whatever your heart desires.

Practice

1 Sit on a cushion or chair in your meditation space. Light a candle and place it on your altar. Invite your higher power to join you in this meditation and guide you in your effort to manifest whatever you wish, however small or significant.

2 Think of what it is you would like to manifest. Ask your higher power that this thing or relationship or project be for the benefit of all beings, including yourself. Ask that this selfless motivation guide all your decisions and activities regarding the project.

When you manifest your dreams for the highest good, you manifest them not only for yourself, but the entire planet. For example, if you want to start a business and your motivation is simply to make a lot of money, this may or may not be for the highest good of all. Or if you want to manufacture something that may harm the environment, you may want to reconsider your options. Instead, imagine starting a company that will help all beings as well as yourself. In this way, with compassionate motivation, you align yourself with the energies of the universe.

3 Visualize that your dream has manifested. What would it look like? How would it feel? If it is a business, see yourself in your office having a meeting with your employees. If you want to run for office, envision yourself giving a campaign speech. Now that it is a reality, is your dream in line with your highest ideals and for the benefit of all?

4 If your dream is indeed for the highest good of all, and you want it to become a reality, write it down and place it in a silver box on your altar. Ask your higher power to help you make it a reality.

BURIED TREASURE

When you were young you may have had many exciting dreams. As you got older, and took on more responsibilities, perhaps getting married, having children and working to pay the bills, you may have set aside those dreams. Meditate on this buried treasure and see where it takes you.

Benefits

- Reconnects you with unfulfilled dreams

- Helps you regard unfulfilled dreams as a treasure

- Expands your vision for your life

When you were a kid, did you want to be a fireman, a musician, a painter or a writer? Maybe you wanted to climb a mountain. What dreams did you have that may have been buried over time?

Meditation

When

Try this meditation if you want to enliven your life.

Preparation

Write about the dreams and interests you had as a child.

Practice

1 Stretch out on a mat on the floor. Cover yourself with a blanket if you think you may need one. Breathe deeply for a few minutes and relax your entire body from head to toe.

2 Recall what you wrote in preparation for this meditation. Choose the dream from your childhood that holds the most resonance for you. Don't worry if it seems childish or impossible. If you wanted to be Superman or Wonder Woman, great. If you wanted to be a musician or raise horses, don't reject it because you think it has nothing to do with your life today.

3 Visualize being or doing what you wished for as a child. Explore the qualities of your life if you were to live your dream. Would you be outdoors, involved with animals, rescuing people? Does this dream still excite you?

4 Now imagine a way to bring at least a part of your dream into your adult life. For example, if you wanted to raise horses, go riding this weekend. If you wanted to be Wonder Woman, consider volunteering and be a hero for kids in need. If you wanted to be a musician, start taking those piano lessons.

5 End your meditation by committing to bring energy to your life by reviving your childhood passions.

SOUL WORK

What is it that you are meant to do in this lifetime? What is your special contribution? Try a little soul work to explore these very important questions.

Benefits

- Helps you concentrate on important questions

- Supports you in bids to manifest your life's work

- Encourages you to express your highest self

Does your work feed your soul? If money was no object, how would you spend your days? What work would make you leap out of bed in the morning, keen to start your day?

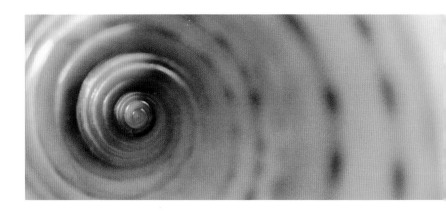

Meditation

When

Practise this meditation if you feel you are at a crossroads in your life and need to do something new.

Preparation

Consider then write down what you care about most deeply and what excites you most intensely.

Practice

1 Sit on a cushion or chair in your meditation space. Light a candle and incense to affirm the importance of this moment and the Sacredness of your life. Meditate by watching your breath for a few minutes in order to calm your mind and relax your body.

2 Read out loud what you wrote in preparation for this meditation. You may have written that you care most about your family, world peace or the environment. Perhaps science lights a fire in your soul. Let yourself feel any emotions that arise. Are you excited, sad, angry? Did you let your family talk you out of working for a park service because it didn't have the prestige they felt you should aspire to? Do you spend enough time with your loved ones?

3 Contemplate how you are living your life today and whether it honours what you have written in your statement. There is no fault here, just awareness. Knowing what you care about and what excites you will start you on the path to a more fulfilled life.

SPIRIT OF PLACE

Are you happy where you are living? Would another location suit you better? This meditation helps you explore the right location for you – body and spirit.

Benefits

- Helps you find the right place to live

- Encourages you to consider body and soul

- Helps you assess where you are currently residing

Do you love the ocean, the mountains or the desert? Do you feel best in big cities or smaller towns? How important is your community to your sense of well-being? Where have you dreamed of living? Are you happy right where you are? These are important questions to help you determine the best place for you to put down roots.

Meditation

When

Try this meditation if you would like to feel more connected to where you live.

Preparation

Write about your ideal place to live. Don't worry if it seems impossible or impractical for you.

Practice

1 Stretch out on a mat on the floor. Make yourself comfortable. Cover yourself with a blanket if you need to. Breathe deeply for a few minutes and relax all your muscles right through from your toes to your crown.

2 Visualize your ideal place to live. Describe the town or city or countryside. Is it a large urban area or a small town? Is it in the country in which you now live or somewhere else in the world? What do the buildings look like?

3 Now describe the weather. Is your ideal place in a warmer climate, a temperate one or in a colder region? Imagine yourself dressed appropriately in this place. Describe the people who live in your ideal place. Are they older, younger, progressive, conservative, intellectuals or sports-minded?

4 What sort of house are you living in? Is it large, small, picturesque, cosy, impressive or modest? Who are you living with? What else about this place is important to you? Why does this place nurture your body and soul?

5 If you already live in your ideal place, feel grateful for that fact. If you would like to move somewhere else, repeat this meditation until you find your place of spirit.

SOUL-MATE

A soul-mate can be your spouse or a friend. He or she is someone you love deeply, who understands and shares your spiritual journey.

Benefits

- Encourages you to find your soul-mate
- Helps you be a soul-mate for someone else
- Helps you know your soul-mate when you meet him or her

A soul-mate is a person with whom you may have worked for many lifetimes on the same path of spiritual development. You may have a great physical attraction to this person or you may feel he or she is like your brother or sister. Having a soul-mate allows you to feel that you are pilgrims on the same path together.

Meditation

When

If you want to attract a soul-mate, practise this meditation for 30 days.

Preparation

Write your spiritual autobiography to better understand your own spiritual journey. Trace your beliefs and spiritual development from the time you were a child until now.

Practice

1 Stretch out on a mat on the floor. Make yourself comfortable, breathe deeply and relax fully.

2 Review the main points of your spiritual autobiography in your mind. Concentrate on where you are now on your spiritual path. What do you believe is your spiritual path and what spiritual work do you envision for yourself now and in the future?

3 Visualize meeting your soul-mate. Are they male or female? Are you meeting at a coffee shop or a social event? What do they look like and what qualities do they possess? Are they sensitive, intelligent, uplifting, generous?

4 Imagine that you have known him or her for lifetimes. Understand this is a reunion rather than a first meeting. Know the person is your spiritual partner, engaged in the same spiritual labour as yourself. Imagine each of you supporting the other as you fulfill your spiritual destiny. Feel blessed to have someone who is a friend whom you trust and who trusts you, with whom you share a true commitment to spiritual work, as well as tenderness and devotion.

5 End your meditation by asking your higher power to help you meet this person in the near future.

SPIRIT HOUSE

Your home, whether it is a house or a rented apartment, can be a special place for reflection, meditation, ritual and ceremony. This meditation will help you create a living space that is a sacred sanctuary for your soul.

Benefits

- Helps you create a nurturing living space
- Encourages you to honour your spirit
- Helps you create sacred space

You may want your house or apartment to be warm, nurturing, beautiful and sacred. Instead, it may be an uninviting and chaotic dumping place for yourself and your possessions. Transform it by meditating on how you would change it.

Meditation

When

Try this meditation if you want to transform your living space to reflect the fact that you are a spiritual being.

Preparation

Walk through your living space, visiting each room. Assess how each room makes you feel – physically, mentally, emotionally and spiritually.

Practice

1 After surveying your home, sit down on a cushion or chair in your meditation space. Close your eyes and breathe deeply for a few minutes.

2 If you are not happy with how your home looks or feels, imagine it the way you would like it to be. If you have created a small sacred space for meditation, consider how you can make your entire home sacred. How can you decorate and arrange your home to reflect your desire for comfort, serenity, warmth or whatever else you need? How can your space honour your spirit? How can you create a home for your soul?

3 Imagine that you are in your spirit house; how would it look and feel? How does it differ from where you live now? How does it nourish your soul? What would you have to do to transform your current living space? Does it require painting, rearranging the furniture and lighting, or cleaning?

4 Repeat this meditation daily for a week before making any changes in your environment. When you begin to make changes, go slowly and engage your body, mind and spirit.

MAKE THE LEAP

You may want to manifest your dreams, but fear may be holding you back. Try this meditation to help you take the leap and make your vision a reality.

Benefits

- Helps identify the fears holding you back

- Moves focus from fear to excitement

- Encourages you to take chances

Meditation

When

Try this meditation if you feel ready to manifest a dream, but are afraid to move forward.

Preparation

Write about what you want to manifest in your life and what is holding you back from doing so.

Practice

1 Sit on a cushion or chair in your meditation space. Meditate by watching your breath for five minutes.

2 Bring to mind a dream you would like to manifest. Ask yourself why you have not moved forward to make it a reality. Explore your beliefs about yourself and how they may be getting in your way.

You may have been held back by unconscious and conscious decisions you have made about what you can handle safely, what you can create practically or what you deserve realistically. Your freedom to grow and manifest your dreams depends on you remaking those limiting decisions, mindsets and self-images.

3 For example, if you have always wanted to learn to ride a horse but are afraid of getting hurt or you feel it is too extravagant for your lifestyle or more fun than you deserve, then examine those beliefs and counter them with new ones. As an example, tell yourself millions of people ride horses without getting hurt, it is money well spent on something that feeds your soul, and of course you deserve to be happy and enjoy your life.

4 End your meditation by committing to taking the first step towards making your dream a reality. It may mean a phone call, doing research, signing up for a class or quitting your job. Whatever it is make sure you make the leap into your future and your happiness.

PROCRASTINATION

You cannot manifest your dreams if you have a habit of procrastinating. Procrastination is simply a bad habit you can overcome with a little effort.

Benefits

- Exposes the fear behind procrastination
- Supports you in breaking the procrastination habit
- Helps you develop positive discipline

It is important to understand why you procrastinate. You could be procrastinating out of fear or because what you plan to do is not in line with what you truly want. You could have a habit of not doing something if you are not in the mood or if you are feeling overwhelmed. This meditation will help you understand why you are procrastinating and imagine how your life would be if you didn't.

Meditation

When

Try this meditation to help you break your procrastination habit.

Preparation

Write down three reasons why you procrastinate in order to make yourself conscious of why you put off doing what you have to do.

Practice

1 Sit on a cushion or chair in your meditation space. Read the three reasons why you procrastinate. For example, you may have written that you are afraid of failing or you are so disorganized that you are overwhelmed all the time. Or you may wait until the last minute to complete a project because you need the pressure to get you going. Try to think about the real reasons why you procrastinate rather than your excuses.

2 Consider each of the three reasons you procrastinate. They may be relieving your stress in the short term, but in the long term, they are undermining you.

3 Now visualize and feel what it would be like if you didn't hesitate before starting a task. Imagine what you could accomplish in your life if you were not a procrastinator. See your productivity and creativity soar. Feel the sense of accomplishment you would have if you worked hard every day and met your deadlines and responsibilities with ease and competence.

4 Commit to being aware of the reasons why you procrastinate and work to overcome them.

SPIRITUAL DECISION-MAKING

Manifesting your dreams usually involves you making many decisions. This meditation will help you to bring a spiritual perspective to your deliberations.

Benefits

- Helps you make the best decisions
- Encourages tapping into your higher self
- Integrates the spiritual and the material

Decisions can be stressful and difficult, but less so if you engage your higher power in the process. Expanding your scope to include the effect of your decision on your soul and your spirit, helps you make decisions that are right for you and right for the universe.

Meditation

When

Try this meditation before bed if you have an important decision to make.

Preparation

Write about the issues involved in your upcoming decision.

Practice

1 Sit on a cushion or chair in your meditation space. Light a candle and invoke the presence of your higher power, whomever or whatever it is. Ask for help in making the decision you are about to consider.

2 Bring to mind the decision you need to make. For example, it could be a decision about whether or not to take a new job that has been offered to you.

3 Go over in your mind the material issues such as salary, status and advancement in your career. Then ask yourself how this job will affect your spirit and your soul. For example, will you be around people who are positive and work well with others? Is the physical environment healthy? Will this work bless

and serve the world? Will this job be more stressful than the one you currently have? How will this job affect your family and social life? Is this job compatible with your spiritual beliefs and your sense of the meaning and purpose of your life?

4 Ask your higher power to help you answer these questions. Sit quietly and continue to consider the questions that are important to you in making this decision. Don't worry if the answers are not readily apparent.

5 End your meditation and sleep on the issues before you make your decision. Let the power of your subconscious mind begin to work on the answers. Look for more clarity about the issue when you awaken.

DREAM MAP

Create a dream map for manifesting your dreams. Then meditate on your map to help your dreams come true.

Benefits

- Encourages visualization of your dreams
- Engages your creativity
- Focuses your mind on making your dreams happen

You see your dreams in your mind first, before you manifest them on the physical plane. Creating a visual map of the things you want to do, have and be, programmes them into your subconscious mind. Seeing your dreams on a daily basis reminds you to take steps to make them a reality. There are no rules for how to create your dream map, except that the images have to mean something to you.

Meditation

When

Create a dream map when you are ready to act on your dreams.

Preparation

Find a stack of old magazine, brochures or other visual material. You will need a base for your map, a plain piece of paper the size you want your map to be. Then you will need scissors and glue. If you want to use other art supplies, gather those as well. Start finding images that symbolize what you would like to manifest in your life.

Practice

1 Find a quiet place where you can be alone. Spread out your materials on a table or on the floor.

2 Sit quietly for a few minutes, breathe deeply and open your heart and mind to your deepest desires. Ask your higher power to help you manifest dreams that are beneficial not only to you, but to the rest of the universe.

3 You may want to divide your dream map into areas, such as spiritual, physical, work, relationships or in any way that makes sense to you. Begin to arrange and paste down images that will serve as a reminder of your dreams. Draw, paint, add glitter or anything else that works for you.

4 When you have finished, ask your higher power to help you manifest the dreams you have visualized on your dream map. Place your dream map on a wall where you can see it every day. If you want to keep it private, put it in a drawer, but take it out every day, look at it and take action towards making your dreams come true.

TAKE THE NEXT STEP

Manifesting your dreams requires having a plan and performing a series of actions. This meditation will help you know the next step to take on your journey.

Benefits

- Helps you keep on track
- Encourages thoughtful decision-making
- Helps you to know the next step

Your dreams manifest through your actions. You perform a series of mental, physical or spiritual tasks, which eventually create the reality you desire. In the beginning, the road to your dreams may seem daunting. This meditation will help you know how to proceed.

Meditation

When

Try this meditation when you want to know what steps to take to realize your dream.

Preparation

You will need a large sheet of paper and marking pens.

Practice

1 Find a place indoors where you can be alone and undisturbed. Sit at a table with your drawing materials in front of you.

2 Close your eyes and visualize a dream you would like to make a reality. For example, if you want to start a vegetarian restaurant, see yourself in your restaurant greeting your guests.

3 Draw a circle in the middle of your paper and write your dream in the centre of it. Now begin to brainstorm all the tasks you have to complete in order to realize your dream. Draw lines running from the centre to other circles, each with a separate task and connect 'sub-tasks' to those tasks. For example, if you need training, make that one task.

Connected to that task you may have 'sub-tasks' of getting a student loan and finding a good training school. Another task may be to visit the best vegetarian restaurants in the country.

4 Fill your paper with every task you can think of that will help you manifest your dream. When you are finished you will have an organic form that looks like a flower or a snowflake. Now begin to prioritize the tasks in a sequence that makes sense to you.

5 Close your eyes again and visualize yourself going through all the steps in sequence, eventually arriving at the same visualization you had before your brainstorming process.

FOLLOW YOUR BLISS

What makes you feel most alive? What excites you more than anything else? This meditation will help you follow your bliss as you make decisions about your life.

Benefits

- Helps you zoom in on what most excites you

- Encourages you to follow your bliss

- Reduces fear of living fully

Following your bliss means letting true joy be your compass. It means more than mere happiness or satisfaction of desire; it means living out your unique nature and divine potential. When you follow your bliss you disregard all the rules that tell you how to live and you seek your own authentic path.

Meditation

When

Try this meditation when you want more out of life.

Preparation

Recall moments of real joy in your life.

Practice

1 Sit on a cushion or chair in your meditation space. Meditate on your breath for five minutes.

2 Recall a moment in your life when you experienced real joy. Imagine you are living that moment all over again. How do you feel? How is this experience different from your ordinary experience?

3 Contemplate the idea that you could live your life in such a way that you always love your experience. How can you make decisions in your life that might make this a reality? For example, if you really hate your job, consider leaving it and exploring what might lead you to joy. Imagine living your dreams and not settling for security or other peoples' approval. How would that feel? Is that thought scary, exciting or both? Do you know why you are alive and what you were born to do?

4 Even if it seems outrageous and impossible, imagine living each moment in pure joy. Imagine savouring each moment, regardless of what life brings. Contemplate the possibility and what you might do to make that happen. Decide on small steps you can take to bring more joy and bliss into your life.

5 End by meditating on your breath for a few minutes.

LET GO OF YOUR PAST

Your past may be dragging you down and getting in the way of you manifesting your dreams. Try this meditation to let go of old emotional and mental baggage.

Benefits

- Helps you identify outdated ideas about yourself

- Helps you let go of the past

- Encourages you to move forward

You may be hanging on to the pain of a lover who dumped you or the humiliation of losing your job or the scars of your less-than-ideal childhood. These events hurt, but they happened in the past. Keeping the past alive – whether in the form of old hurts, outdated ideas or useless habits – makes it difficult for you to be open to new relationships and new opportunities in the present.

Meditation

When

Try this meditation if you feel stuck in a painful past.

Preparation

Write down those things that happened long ago that still cause pain when you think about them.

Practice

1 Stretch out on a mat on the floor. Cover yourself with a light blanket if you need to. Breathe deeply and relax for a few minutes.

2 Bring to mind any emotional baggage from your past. Maybe your partner abandoned you for your best friend. If you still feel pangs of anger and humiliation years later, it is time to let it go. Visualize your emotions as an old, beat-up suitcase you drag around wherever you go. When your lover left you, you were hurting and needed to process your pain. But years later, these old feelings no longer serve you. Imagine letting go of the suitcase and your old pain. Feel how much lighter you feel.

3 Continue scanning your memory for old baggage – old worn-out emotions and ideas that no longer serve you. Visualize them as old pieces of luggage, some with broken handles, strapped up with tape. Thank them for all the service they have given, but let them know it's time for you to let them go.

4 Visualize and feel yourself as lighter, unencumbered and free. Breathe deeply and relax for a few minutes. See your future opening before you, full of promise and opportunity.

TRAVELLER

Have you always wanted to travel, but settled for armchair travel with the help of travel books? This meditation will help you make your desire to travel a reality.

Benefits

- Helps you get where you want to go

- Encourages you to act on your desires

- Helps you see that anything is possible

Do you have stacks of old travel magazines in your basement? Chances are you are a traveller at heart. But if your fears are getting in the way, you may be cheating yourself out of your dreams.

Meditation

When

Try this meditation if you want to travel but somehow never get around to it.

Preparation

Write down all the places you would like to visit before your die. Rank them in order of importance to you.

Practice

1 Stretch out on a mat on the floor. Cover yourself with a light blanket. Breathe deeply for a few minutes and clear your mind.

2 Pick the first travel destination on your list. Review the reasons why you have never travelled to that place. Perhaps you don't have enough money, enough time or you have young children that need care. Perhaps it seems beyond your capacity, a little scary, more than you deserve. Check to see if your thoughts may be holding you back.

3 Visualize yourself in your dream location. It may be Bombay, New York, London or the Amazon Rain Forest. It could be a small town in Ireland where your grandmother was born or Cape Town, South Africa. See yourself walking down a street, taking in the sights and the people. Notice what you are wearing and who is with you. Feel your excitement and joy at actually being in your dream destination.

4 Commit to taking a step towards making your dream come true. For example, order travel brochures and check out prices. Research ways that you might volunteer your time and get a reduced or free trip. Check out exchanging houses with a family from a different country. Actively work to remove the obstacles to manifesting your dream travel.

5 End your meditation by resting quietly for a few more minutes.

CONNECTING
TO THE DIVINE

MEDITATIONS FOR CONNECTING TO THE DIVINE

This last section brings you meditations inspired by a variety of spiritual traditions, both Eastern and Western, which help you experience the Sacred or the Divine. These meditations introduce you to, or deepen your own notion of something, or some being, greater than yourself. They are designed to spark your imagination, expand your understanding of the Divine and help you to contemplate the meaning of the Sacred in your life.

You will begin with 'Four directions,' a meditation that introduces you to a ritual for creating a sacred environment. 'Spider Woman' draws on the Native American tradition and teaches you how to use myth for meditation and spiritual development. Moving on to Japan, 'Amaterasu, the sun goddess' inspires you to overcome wounding and give your gifts to the world. With 'Buddha nature' you contemplate your own Buddha nature in the form of a seed. If you are Catholic or curious about Catholicism, try 'Rosary' and learn how to meditate on this beautiful set of prayers.

Quakers practise waiting in silence for the presence of God. Have your own 'Friends' meeting with 'Quaker way'. 'Devotion' will give you a direct experience of Divine love, while the 'Path of grace' will help you access Divine grace in your everyday life. The Goddess has many names: 'Divine feminine' introduces you to the Divine in female form. 'Jesus the Saviour' helps you understand the way of Christ and 'The four noble truths' help you understand the way of the Buddha.

Learn to meditate on the famous prayer of St Francis of Assisi by practising the meditation named for him. If you are attracted to Jewish mysticism you will enjoy the 'Wisdom of the Kabbalah,' and if you are attracted to Islamic mysticism, then 'The Sufi way' is for you. Often the most challenging spiritual paths involve the help or guidance of a teacher. 'Spiritual teacher' will help you choose the right one for you.

To find your animal totem and spirit guide, try 'The Wiccan way'. 'Reconnecting with the Divine' is a wonderful meditation for coming home to yourself and the Sacred. 'Directed prayer' and 'Non-directed prayer' teach you two very powerful forms of prayer. If you feel your god is absent, use 'Divine Presence' to confirm it is not. 'Shiva's dance' introduces you to the Hindu understanding of the Sacred. Finally, 'Personal God vs mystical reality' helps you meditate on your understanding of the Divine in your life.

FOUR DIRECTIONS

Many spiritual traditions invoke the four cardinal directions in their prayers and rituals. This meditation introduces you to this practice.

Benefits

- Introduces you to a powerful spiritual tool

- Helps ground you physically and psychologically

- Helps you connect with your environment

The four cardinal directions are north, south, east and west. In Buddhist, Native American, Wicca and other spiritual traditions, the spiritual practitioner creates a sacred circle or environment by invoking the centre and four directions. This particular meditation honours the directions and the five elements of the Tibetan Buddhist tradition.

Meditation

When

Practise this meditation when you want to ground yourself in your environment.

Preparation

Find a place outdoors where you will not be disturbed. Bring a compass in order to determine direction.

Practice

1 Locate the cardinal directions using your compass. Stand with your spine straight. Take a deep breath. Visualize inhaling your breath into your heart. Exhale very slowly. Feel your heart expand and fill with warmth as you take another deep breath and exhale very slowly. Continue breathing in this way for a few minutes.

2 Now stand facing east. Offer thanks to the east for the water you drink, bathe in and cook with.

3 Rotate to stand facing south. Offer thanks to the south for the Earth and the food you eat.

4 Stand facing west. Offer thanks to the west for fire and the warmth it provides, and its transformative powers.

5 Stand facing north and from your heart, offer thanks to the north for the air you breathe.

6 Now bring your focus to the centre where you are standing. Offer thanks for the environment in which you live. Take a moment to enjoy the state of gratitude you have evoked. Take a deep breath into your heart and exhale.

SPIDER WOMAN

Spider Woman is a Native American goddess or deity. This beautiful meditation introduces you to the power of myth to invoke spiritual understanding.

Benefits

- Introduces you to a Native American spirituality

- Helps you understand interconnectedness

- Introduces you to the power of myth

Long before the universe existed, lonely Spider Woman sat down to think. Suddenly she had an idea. She was the weaver so she set up her loom and began to weave. As she wove a star appeared every time one thread crossed another; before long she had woven thousands of stars. Each one was tied to every other one in the

Meditation

When

Try this meditation to explore myth for spiritual growth.

Preparation

Read the Spider Woman myth.

Practice

1 Sit on a cushion or chair and meditate on the Spider Woman myth for ten minutes.

2 Write a paragraph about what the myth taught you.

web. She stopped and looked at it, but it was not quite what she wanted. She chose one star that had planets circling around it. She chose one of those planets that had bright blue oceans and sparkling white clouds, and set up her loom on that planet. This time as she wove, a living thing appeared whenever one thread crossed another. She wove plants, birds, fish and insects into her web. She wove all of the animals. And every one of these living things was connected to everything on her web. Then she stopped weaving to look at it. There was still something missing.

She started to weave again, and this time human beings – men, women and children – appeared at the crossing threads. And each human being that she wove into her Great Web was connected to every other thing: to the other animals, to the plants, to the mountains, seas and deserts, even to the distant stars. Every human being – and indeed everything that Spider Woman wove into her Great Web – is connected to every other thing. Spider Woman was pleased and continues to weave to this day.

AMATERASU, THE SUN GODDESS

Amaterasu is an ancient sun goddess of the Shinto religion. Meditation on her may help you recover from abuse.

Amaterasu was born from the left eye of the primeval being Izanagi. When her brother Susanowo abused her, she decided to hide in the cave of heaven and closed the entrance with an enormous stone. She had lost her confidence and her ability to love.

Benefits

- Introduces you to the Japanese Shinto religion

- Helps you overcome wounding

- Encourages you to give your gifts to the world

Meditation

When

Try this meditation when you feel wounded and withdrawn.

Preparation

Read the Amaterasu myth.

Practice

1 Sit on a cushion or chair in your meditation space. Meditate on the Amaterasu myth and what it means to you for ten minutes.

2 Write about what you have learned.

Thus darkness surrounded the world and people huddled in their homes, listless and hopeless. Without her light, they could not see their own strength and lost the will to live. In despair, some of the gods decided to entice Amaterasu out of the cave by throwing a party.

They placed a large mirror at the mouth of the cave and decorated the trees. Uzume, the goddess of laughter, began an outrageous dance accompanied by loud music. Hearing the music and the laughter, Amaterasu peered outside to see what was going on.

As soon as she saw her own brilliant and beautiful reflection in the mirror, it was as if she was seeing herself for the first time. She immediately returned to her palace and vowed never again to withdraw from life. She asked that mirrors be hung in the doorways to her temples, so that all who passed by might look deeply into them. The elders say that after Amaterasu returned, the people of Japan and the gods themselves carried on their lives with renewed courage and joy.

BUDDHA NATURE

Buddhism teaches that you have Buddha nature. In other words, you have the capacity to become enlightened and become a Buddha yourself.

Benefits

- Introduces you to Buddhism
- Encourages you to develop spiritually
- Promotes self-responsibility

A Buddha is a person who has developed all the positive qualities possible and has eliminated all negativity. The historical Buddha, Shakyamuni or Gautama Buddha, lived about 2,500 years ago in India. However, he was not the first Buddha, nor will he be the last. He was an 'ordinary' human being before he became enlightened. Enlightenment is often compared to awakening. When you become enlightened, you become all knowing and free of negativity. You become the embodiment of wisdom and compassion. As a Buddha you can be of tremendous help to others.

Meditation

When

Try this meditation if you are feeling negative about yourself or your potential to develop spiritually.

Preparation

If possible, read the life story of the historical Buddha, Shakyamuni, at your library or on the Web.

Practice

1 Sit on a cushion or chair in your meditation space. Meditate on your breath for five minutes.

2 Contemplate your own Buddha nature in the form of a seed. Imagine that you begin to 'water' this seed with meditation on patience, love, compassion and other positive topics. Imagine that you strive to be a more positive, loving and compassionate person. Now you have what is called a 'growing Buddha nature'.

3 Over time see yourself slowly eliminating your negative habits and replacing them with positive ones. Imagine your thoughts and actions becoming more positive every day. Imagine how it would be to become a Buddha, to be enlightened.

4 Imagine having no negativity, no suffering and perfect wisdom and compassion. Imagine being able to help all beings. Sit quietly and contemplate what that might be like.

5 If you choose, commit to growing your own Buddha nature by increasing your positive virtues and eliminating your negative habits.

ROSARY

Catholics have been saying the rosary or using prayer beads to meditate since the twelfth century. When saying the rosary, you recite the 'Our Father' and 'Hail Mary' prayers while meditating on one of the mysteries of the liturgy.

Benefits

- Introduces you to Catholic meditation practice
- Introduces you to the Catholic mysteries
- Teaches Catholic prayers

The Catholic rosary is made up of five sets of ten beads with five large beads in between. The 'Our Father' is recited for the large beads and the 'Hail Mary' is recited for the smaller beads. For each 'decade' of beads you complete, you then meditate on one of the 'mysteries'.

Our Father Who art in heaven, Hallowed be Thy Name. Thy Kingdom come, Thy Will be done, On earth as it is in Heaven. Give us this day, our daily bread, And forgive us our trespasses, as we forgive those who trespass against us. And lead us not into temptation, but deliver us from evil. Amen.

Hail Mary, Full of Grace, The Lord is with thee. Blessed art thou among women, and blessed is the fruit of thy womb, Jesus. Holy Mary, Mother of God, pray for us sinners now, and at the hour of death. Amen.

Meditation

When

It is recommended that you pray the rosary in the morning and evening.

Preparation

Borrow or buy a Catholic rosary. Read over and, if possible, memorize the 'Our Father' and 'Hail Mary'.

Practice

1 Sit on a cushion or chair in your meditation space. Or if you prefer, kneel before your altar.

2 Begin saying the rosary by reciting an 'Our Father' when your fingers touch a large bead and a 'Hail Mary' when your fingers touch a small bead.

3 As you say the rosary, meditate on the life and mysteries of Christ as you understand them. Remember Mary and the birth of Christ, and Christmas as we celebrate it in the Joyful mysteries. The Luminous mysteries focus on the life and teachings of Christ, which concentrated on love and compassion. The Sorrowful mysteries remind us of the crucifixion and death of Christ, symbolizing sacrifice and surrender to God. And finally, the Glorious mysteries celebrate the resurrection and ascension of Christ into heaven.

QUAKER WAY

George Fox started the Quaker movement in England in the seventeenth century. Followers of this movement call themselves 'Friends' or 'Friends of Jesus'. The name 'Quaker' was given to them by others who said they quaked with religious zeal.

Benefits

- Introduces you to Quaker meditation

- Promotes a direct relationship with God

- Encourages community

Quakers worship by gathering two or more people together, being still and seeking God's presence. By attentively waiting together in silence, Friends find peace of mind and a renewed sense of purpose for living in tune with God's will.

Meditation

When

Try this meditation on a weekly basis with friends or family.

Preparation

Enlist one or more friends or family members who would like to sit in meditation with you.

Practice

1 Sit facing your friends on chairs or cushions. Together, settle into a quiet space and seek God's presence and will. Let the silence remove any pressure or anxiety you may feel from your daily life. Try to accept yourself exactly as you are and be released from fear, confusion and selfishness. Try to be open to God as well as to each other. Be aware that your intention in listening and waiting in this way is to meet God directly.

2 You may mediate and worship in this way without words, but if you or anyone else present cares to, you can express aloud your experience. Be open and accepting of whatever is said. For example, you may speak about how the teachings of Jesus touch your life or refer to personal experience. Try to receive what others say in a positive way and look for the underlying truth.

3 Contemplate what is essential and eternal rather than trivial. If you speak, express yourself simply and with respect. Look for Truth by sitting quietly and waiting for your heart to open to God's message.

4 End your meditation session whenever your group feels ready.

DEVOTION

There are many spiritual traditions that rely on devotion as a path to spiritual fulfillment. Use this meditation to explore devotion as a direct experience of Divine love.

Benefits

- Introduces you to the practice of devotion

- Helps you bring devotion into your spiritual path

- Empowers you to grow spiritually

The practice of devotion as a spiritual path is a way to direct mystical experience. To be devoted means to engage with love.

Meditation

When

If you feel your ego is getting in the way of following a spiritual path, try meditating on devotion.

Preparation

Think about a time when you have felt devotion in your life.

Practice

1 Sit on a cushion or chair in your meditation space. If you have an altar, make offerings to your personal God, teacher or higher power by lighting a candle or incense and making offerings of flowers or food.

2 Meditate on relinquishing your attachment to superficial concerns that may be getting in the way of your spiritual path. For example, if you are obsessed with clothes and how you look, you may contemplate how this may not be serving you spiritually.

3 Immerse yourself in unselfish, unceasing love for the Divine. On a devotional path everything is an expression of God's love. Your stress, pain and anxiety arise from not seeing

the world or yourself as worthy of love. Let go of your ego's painful struggle for recognition and dominance and surrender to Divine love.

4 Imagine every breath you take in is love, and every breath out is compassion. You are an expression of God's love and his or her love flows through you every moment.

5 Consider forming a relationship with a teacher, in whatever form he or she takes. Imagine you are devoted to your teacher and the teachings which empower you to develop on your spiritual path.

6 End your session by meditating on how you might practise devotion in your current spiritual path.

PATH OF GRACE

Grace is at the heart of the Christian tradition. It is God's grace that allows forgiveness and new beginnings. This meditation helps you bring God's grace into your everyday life.

Benefits

- Helps you rejoice in God's forgiveness

- Encourages you to extend grace into your personal life

- Helps encourage hope and resilience

You may be familiar with one of the most famous Christian hymns called 'Amazing Grace'. John Newton, a reformed slave trader, wrote the words in 1779. He says 'Amazing grace! How sweet the sound that saved a wretch like me! I once was lost, but now am found, was blind, but now I see.' Through God's gift of grace and forgiveness, he was able to see the error of his ways and begin a life guided by his wisdom. God's grace is both transformational and healing.

Meditation

When

When you want to turn your life around and live in accord with God's grace, as you understand it.

Preparation

Write about how you have been blessed by God's grace.

Practice

1 Sit on a cushion or chair in your meditation space. Light a candle. Breathe deeply for a few minutes to centre and calm your mind.

2 Contemplate how you can make room for grace in your life. How can you extend the grace you have been given to your family, friends and community? In this world where everything is pushed to its limits and people are emotionally, financially and physically stressed, it is important to help relieve the pressure and create the space for grace to enter. How can you reorganize your priorities so that you can accommodate the needs of your circle for tenderness and grace?

3 Decide on three ways in which you can follow the path of grace. For example, you might invite for dinner a friend with whom you have had a falling-out. Ask your partner how you can be a better partner. Get involved in helping the elderly in your community.

4 End your meditation by composing a prayer to God, thanking Him for all His blessings.

DIVINE FEMININE

The Divine Feminine is an empowering archetype for both men and women. Meditating on her helps you to honour all that is feminine in yourself and others.

Benefits

- Introduces you to the Divine Mother

- Helps you honour the feminine in yourself and others

- Promotes respect for women

The Goddess has many names: Tara, Sofia, Artemis, Athena, Cerridwen, Ceres, Mary, Hestia, Hera, Psyche, Persephone, Isis, Aphrodite, Oshun, Oya, Black Madonna, Guadalupe, Spider Woman, White Buffalo Woman. The list is endless. This meditation introduces you to the Divine Feminine as an object of meditation.

Meditation

When

Try this meditation if you are feeling depressed and suffering from addictions.

Preparation

Study the Goddess in her many forms at the library or on the Web.

Practice

1 Find a quiet place outdoors. Close your eyes and breath deeply for a few minutes.

2 Imagine yourself walking along a pathway that leads into a forest. You come upon a beautiful sanctuary. Slowly you push open the door and enter. On an altar stands a statue of the female deity, the Goddess. She does not belong to any particular religion; she is simply the Mother, God as a woman, the feminine Divine.

3 As you kneel before her, she begins to teach you about the sacred feminine and how to honour her in your life. She stresses the importance of living in the now, the sacredness of your body

and that your being is more important than your personality. Process, she says, is more important than product. All matter is sacred and all matter is energy. Whether you are male or female, your soul is feminine – it is the receiver of the Divine. Life, death and rebirth are the natural cycle of existence.

4 Contemplate what she has taught you for as long as you like.

5 End your meditation by thanking her for her wisdom. Leave the sanctuary and the forest and return to the place you chose for meditation.

JESUS THE SAVIOUR

Jesus Christ's message was one of sacrifice and salvation. Whether you are a practising Christian or not, this meditation will help you connect to your compassionate nature.

Benefits

- Introduces you to Christianity
- Promotes humility
- Helps you understand the idea of salvation

Jesus lived in Palestine from 1 CE to about 33 CE. The name 'Jesus' is from the Hebrew name 'Joshua' and means 'Jehovah is salvation' He is considered both God and human, and the second person of the Holy Trinity of God the Father, God the Son and God the Holy Spirit. He was born to the Virgin Mary, died on the cross to atone for the sins of human beings, rose from the dead and ascended into heaven.

Meditation

When

Try this meditation if you want to understand the meaning of sacrifice in your life.

Preparation

Read the New Testatment of the Bible.

Practice

1 Sit on a cushion or chair in your meditation space. Meditate on your breath for five minutes to calm and centre your mind.

2 Recall the story of Jesus Christ. Contemplate how He sacrificed His life out of love for humans who were living in sin and delusion. Imagine His desire to remove our suffering. Think about how He embodied compassion, forgiveness, love and sacrifice.

3 Think about your own life and how you might live according to Jesus Christ's example. In what ways could you sacrifice your own needs and comforts in order to relieve the suffering of others?

For example, how available are you to your family members and their needs? How could you make life easier for your co-workers? Are you able to forgive others and refrain from judgement? Contemplate these qualities which Christ had and how you might develop them in your own life.

4 Meditate on forgiveness and salvation. Understand that no matter how negative you have been, you have the opportunity to forgive yourself, to be forgiven and start anew.

5 End your meditation by returning to watching your breath for five minutes.

THE FOUR NOBLE TRUTHS

The Four Noble Truths are among the first teachings that Buddha gave after achieving enlightenment. They outline the basic Buddhist path.

Benefits

- Introduces you to the basic Buddhist path

- Conceives of the Divine as Buddhahood

- Shows a way to relieve suffering

The Four Noble Truths are as follows: your current life is suffering; your attachment, anger and ignorance cause your suffering; your suffering can end and you can enter nirvana; you can end your suffering by following an eight-fold path.

Meditation

When

Try this meditation if you are interested in a Buddhist spiritual path.

Preparation

Read about Buddhism at your library or on the Web.

Practice

1 Sit on a cushion or chair in your meditation space. Meditate by watching your breath for five minutes.

2 Meditate on the first truth of suffering. There is the suffering of suffering: illness, pain and other distress. There is the suffering of change: all good things, however great, including your life, come to an end. There is all-pervasive suffering: at every moment you have the potential to suffer. Overall, this truth comments on our chronic dissatisfaction.

3 Contemplate the second truth. Anger is one of the main reasons you cause harm and causing harm has karmic consequences. Attachment keeps you in cyclic *samsara* as you try to relieve your suffering unsuccessfully through worldly activities. Our ignorance gets us in to trouble because we don't understand others or reality.

4 Think about the third truth; how your suffering can end and you can attain the peace of nirvana. The good news is that if you change your own mind, you can make this happen.

5 Contemplate the fourth truth; that there is an eight-fold path that will help you to nirvana. That path is correct thought, correct speech, correct action, correct livelihood, correct understanding, correct effort, correct mindfulness and correct concentration.

6 End your mediation by reviewing the Four Noble Truths.

ST FRANCIS OF ASSISI

St Francis was born in 1182 into a very wealthy family in the small town of Assisi in Italy. Although rich, he decided to devote his life to God. He is known widely for his love of animals, the depressed and the outcast.

Benefits

- Introduces you to a Catholic saint.

- Introduces you to a beautiful prayer to God

- Promotes love and compassion

St Francis went from village to village preaching the love of God. His gospel of kindness and love spread all over Europe. He eventually founded the Order of Mendicant Friars or Franciscans, whose members take a vow of poverty, chastity, love and obedience. This meditation is based on contemplation of the famous Prayer of St Francis.

Meditation

When

Meditate on the prayer of St Francis at the beginning or end of your day.

Preparation

Read the prayer out loud.

Practice

1 Sit on a cushion or chair in your meditation space.

2 Recite the following prayer of St Francis of Assisi and meditate on its meaning for you.

O Lord, make me an instrument of
Thy Peace!
Where there is hatred, let me sow love,
Where there is injury, pardon,
Where there is discord, harmony,
Where there is doubt, faith,
Where there is despair, hope,
Where there is darkness, light, and
Where there is sorrow, joy.
O Divine Master, grant that I may not so much seek to
be consoled as to console,
to be understood as to understand;
to be loved as to love; for it is in giving that we receive;
It is in pardoning that we are pardoned.
and it is in dying that we are born to Eternal Life.

WISDOM OF THE KABBALAH

Kabbalah, a form of Jewish mysticism, teaches meditation as a direct way to experience God. Kabbalistic meditation techniques include visualizing the Divine Name and meditating on sacred words and letters.

Benefits

- Introduces you to Jewish mysticism

- Helps you connect with God or the Divine

- Helps you understand your place in the universe

This meditation is based on the word 'Shema', the Hebrew word for 'hear'. It is the first word of a famous Jewish prayer affirming faith in one God.

Meditation

When

Practise this meditation in the morning to start your day.

Preparation

If possible, learn more about the Kabbalah at your local library or on the Web.

Practice

1 Sit on a cushion or chair in your meditation space. Breathe deeply for a few minutes to calm, centre and focus your body and mind.

2 Inhale silently, and exhale saying 'shh'. Then inhale again silently and exhale saying 'mmm'. Repeat this process for five minutes, allowing it to draw you deeper and deeper into a meditative state.

3 From this calm and focused state, begin to meditate on some of the beliefs of the Kabbalah. Consider that an Infinite Being is the source of all existence.

4 Understand the purpose of your life is to become one with that Infinite Being or the Divine. Become one with the Divine by living a moral and spiritual life. Know that because you are one with all humanity you must be compassionate. Realize you are a microcosm of all creation and made in the image of the Divine.

5 End your session by repeating the 'Shema' meditation for as long as you like.

THE SUFI WAY

Sufism is the inner, mystical, spiritual dimension of Islam that arose around the ninth century. The Sufi works to achieve a state of opening or illumination in union with God.

Benefits

- Introduces you to Sufism

- Promotes mystical union with God

- Helps you to surrender to God's love

In Sufism, the mind is known as 'the slayer of the real' as it separates you from spiritual truth that you only find in your heart. Truth is understood to be a state of oneness with God, beyond the duality of your mind. You meditate by quieting your mind and focusing on God, as if you are a lover seeking your beloved.

Meditation

When

Practise this meditation early in the morning.

Preparation

Think about what surrendering to God's love means to you.

Practice

1 Sit on a cushion or chair in your meditation space. Breathe deeply for a few minutes to relax and prepare to meditate.

2 Focus on your heart and the area of your heart *chakra* at your breastbone. Focus on someone you love. He or she could be a family member, a lover or a friend. Feel whatever feelings emerge. You may feel a warmth, a sweetness, a softness or a tenderness. You may feel a sense of peace or silence. You may feel heartache, pain or loss. Immerse yourself in this feeling and try to place all of yourself in the love within your heart.

3 Thoughts will intrude into your feeling state. Memories may be triggered. Pictures will emerge in your mind's eye. Imagine taking every thought and drowning or merging it into your feelings of love. With practise, all your thoughts will disappear and you will be immersed in your feelings of love.

4 Eventually practise this meditation with God as the object of love. Approach God as a lover longing for his or her Beloved.

SPIRITUAL TEACHER

Spiritual teachers are available in all traditions. It is important to choose a teacher wisely. This meditation will guide you to find the right teacher to help you access the Divine.

Benefits

- Helps you understand the teacher-student relationship

- Helps you assess the teacher's qualities

- Empowers you as a student

Tibetan Buddhists recommend spending years assessing a potential teacher. This is probably good advice for any tradition, whether it is Christian, Buddhist, Hindu or New Age. Do not make the mistake of thinking a teacher will take over responsibility for your life. Ultimately, the responsibility for your spiritual development is yours alone.

Meditation

When

Try this meditation if you are considering a spiritual teacher.

Preparation

Write about why you want a spiritual teacher or guru.

Practice

1 Sit on a cushion or chair in your meditation space. Breathe deeply to relax your body and centre your mind.

2 Ask yourself why you want a spiritual teacher or guru. What do you expect to learn and why do you think one is necessary? Ask yourself if you have the following qualities: are you open-minded? Are you intelligent and do you have a critical mind, willing to question your teacher? Do you want to develop spiritually, not just intellectually?

3 Ask yourself if your potential teacher has the following qualities: is he or she a moral and ethical person who does not harm others? Is he or she able to concentrate? Does he or she appear to be free of ego and selfishness? Does he

or she have love and compassion as the main motivations for teaching? Has your potential teacher realized the highest levels of your tradition? Does he or she have tremendous energy and enthusiasm for teaching? Does he or she have extensive scholarly knowledge in your tradition? Is your potential teacher more spiritually developed than you are? Can he or she communicate well? And finally, has your teacher given up personal disappointment in his or her students?

4 Spend time contemplating the qualities listed above. Your potential teacher doesn't have to have every quality but the first five are the most important.

THE TAOIST WAY

Taoism, along with Confucianism and Buddhism, is one of the three great religions of China. The founder of Taoism is believed to be Lao-Tsu (604–531 BCE), author of the *Tao-te-Ching*.

Benefits

- Introduces you to Taoist thought
- Promotes peace and serenity
- Connects you with nature

Lao-Tsu created a philosophy and way of life that is peaceful and in harmony with nature. Taoism has influenced acupuncture, holistic medicine, meditation and martial arts such as T'ai Chi and Chi Kung. The Yin/Yang is a well-known Taoist symbol showing two curved shapes within a circle, one dark and one light, each containing part of the other. It symbolizes any two dualistic forces, such as light and dark, male and female.

Meditation

When

Practise this mediation when you want to feel more in harmony with nature and others.

Preparation

Find a river or stream.

Practice

1 Sit or stand next to a river or stream at a spot where you can be quiet and undisturbed. Breath deeply for a few minutes to quiet and centre your mind.

2 Notice how the water flows over and around rocks or tree roots. Contemplate how life is more harmonious when you do not resist it or go against it. The Taoist term *wu-wei* means 'not forcing'. It means going with the grain or swimming with the current rather than against it. It means not winning in order to achieve higher goals.

3 Contemplate how you feel when trying to force an issue or make something happen according to your wishes. Even if you get your way, how do you feel being in conflict and competition with others? Was that the best approach for all involved?

4 *Wu-wei* is an approach to life in which you observe the flow of energy in nature and human behaviour and chooses the most harmonious way of dealing with it. Observe the stream and how water flows by choosing the path of least resistance. How can you use this wisdom of nature to make your life and the lives of those around you more peaceful and harmonious?

THE WICCAN WAY

Wicca is a recently created neo-pagan religion that began in the UK in the 1940s and has since spread throughout Europe, Canada and the US. It is loosely based on the symbols, beliefs and deities of ancient Celtic and Druidic societies.

Benefits

- Introduces you to Wicca
- Promotes connection with nature
- Introduces you to your animal spirit guide

Most Wiccan practitioners believe in a male and female form of God. Some are polytheistic. Many choose an animal totem that functions as a spirit guide in their daily life. This meditation introduces you to your animal totem.

Meditation

When

Practise this mediation when you are open to having a spirit guide or animal totem.

Preparation

Have a look at a nature book with beautiful photos of animals. See which ones attract you. Pay attention to your dreams for a week and see if a particular animal appears.

Practice

1 Sit on a cushion or chair in your meditation space. Close your eyes and sit with a straight spine.

2 Imagine yourself in a large field. In the near distance you see mountains; you begin to walk towards them. You come upon the opening to a cave. At the entrance is a lamp, which you pick up, then enter the cave. Your lamp illuminates the warm, dry interior. You sense a benign presence and out of curiosity you step further into cave.

3 You hold up your lamp and look upon the being you have come to see. You recognize this being as your animal totem. Is it a bear, a dog, a rabbit? Is it a horse or a lion? Speak to this animal and let it speak to you in return. Ask what it is there to teach you and how you can incorporate its guidance into your daily life. If you want, ask advice about a specific problem that concerns you.

4 Bow to your new animal guide. Ask for it to tell you its name. Give your animal guide a gift and accept one in return. Ask that he or she be there for you whenever you need guidance. Bow again as you leave. Return the lamp you borrowed at the mouth of the cave. Turn and look back, memorizing the exact location of the cave so that you can return whenever you desire.

RECONNECTING WITH THE DIVINE

If you once had a spiritual life but have let it go, and now feel a little lost and confused, this meditation will help you reconnect with the Divine.

Benefits

- Helps you choose a spiritual path

- Assists you in reconnecting with the Divine

- Encourages you to take your time

Meditation

When

Try this meditation if you want to reconnect with your spirituality.

Preparation

Write a short spiritual autobiography.

Practice

1 Sit on a cushion or chair in your meditation space. Breathe deeply to relax and clear your mind. Ask God or your higher power to join you in this meditation. You may feel uncomfortable or guilty for not having him or her as part of your life for such a long time. Recall that the Divine is all-loving and all-compassionate and by calling on him or her, you will have their assistance.

You may have once belonged to a church and, for whatever reason, left it. Perhaps you had a falling-out with your minister or priest or someone in your church. Or perhaps you no longer felt comfortable with the beliefs and tenets of your chosen faith. Time has passed and you are not sure where to start or what path feels right for you. All you know is that you want to reconnect with God or your higher power. This meditation will help you sort out what you want to do.

2 Read your spiritual autobiography to God or your higher power. Now ask for your relationship to be renewed. Ask for his or her guidance in re-establishing your connection. Sit quietly and ask that this happen.

3 If you feel comfortable, ask for help in choosing a new spiritual path or help in returning to your old one. Allow yourself time for this to emerge. Sit quietly and open your heart to the idea of rejoining a community.

4 End your meditation by thanking God or you higher power for re-entering you life.

DIRECTED PRAYER

In directed prayer you ask God or your higher power for something specific to happen. You might also use affirmations. This form of prayer can be a powerful tool for healing.

Benefits

- Helps you focus on what you are praying for

- Makes use of visualization and intention

- Promotes healing

You are probably most familiar with directed prayer, in which you petition God or a higher power for something specific to happen. For example, if you have a loved one who is sick with cancer, you may ask God to heal that person by removing his or her cancer cells. You also visualize this happening.

Meditation

When

Practise directed prayer when you want
to pray to God or your higher power for
a specific result.

Preparation

Determine if you want to pray for
something to happen for yourself or
someone else.

Practice

1 Sit on a cushion or chair in your
meditation space or if you prefer,
kneel in prayer.

2 Bring to mind what you want to pray
for. Be specific. If you want to pray
for your own healing, ask God or your
higher power to restore your health. For
example, if you have a thyroid imbalance,
pray that your medication will work and
you will feel healthy again.

3 Petition God from your heart.
Visualize your illness being removed
through Divine love and intervention.
See your medication working in your
blood stream, altering your hormones
and giving your tired thyroid a boost.

4 Practise this directed prayer on a
daily basis until you feel some
improvement. When this happens, thank
God or your higher power for his or her
kind intervention.

NON-DIRECTED PRAYER

Non-directed prayer is open-ended. Although it is directed to God or your higher power, it does not ask for a specific outcome to happen or a goal to be realized.

Benefits

- Offers an alternative to directed prayer

- Introduces a powerful form of prayer

- Introduces you to the power of the mind

Meditation

When

Meditate using non-directed prayer any time.

Preparation

Be open and receptive to the power of prayer in your life.

Practice

1 Sit on a cushion or chair in your meditation space. Meditate on your breath for five minutes in order to calm and centre your mind.

2 Think of a person, either yourself or someone else, you would like to help through prayer. Bring to mind the

In non-directed prayer, you pray by saying and intending 'Thy will be done' or 'Let it be'. In doing so, you align yourself with Divine Mind. Consider the outcome you want as an accomplished fact but do not mentally specify how to arrive at the outcome.

problem you would like to address. For example, you may want to heal a rash that appeared for an unknown reason.

3 Generate a feeling of love and compassion for yourself and others. Ask God or your higher power to restore you to a state of balance in line with his or her desire, whatever that may be. Instead of asking for a specific outcome

which has been visualized and defined by you, pray that the principles, patterns and conditions which are best for you in this particular situation be manifested. Ask that they be in line with Divine will and for the good of all.

4 Practise this non-directed prayer on a daily basis until your condition or circumstance improves.

DIVINE PRESENCE

You may have the sense that God or the Divine is absent, so you pray that he or she may make themselves known. Yet God, the Divine or the Sacred, however you characterize him, her or it, is intimately present in every moment.

Benefits

- Challenges the notion that God is absent

- Encourages the view that all life is part of the Sacred

- Helps you recognize Divine energy

The Divine is present as an energy that sustains you. The spiritual journey is often understood as the purification of illusion. One of the main illusions of our time is materialism or a view that limits reality to only that which can be ascertained by the senses. This meditation will help you reanimate your reality with the presence of the Sacred.

Meditation

When

Try this meditation when you want to recognize the Divine presence in your life.

Preparation

Explore your understanding of the sacredness of all reality.

Practice

1 Sit on a cushion or chair in your meditation space. Breathe deeply for a few minutes in order to focus and centre your mind.

2 Ask that God or the Divine be with you. Realize, as you ask, that the Divine is continuously present. Meditate on the idea that the Divine is with you at all times and you actually don't really need to invoke him or her. Ask for the Divine to be with you only to bring him or her into your consciousness. You do this because you forget, in your ordinary daily life, that God or the Divine dwells within you.

3 Contemplate the idea that God or the Divine dwells within all creation. Divine energy animates the universe, from the lowliest quark to the endless reaches of space. It is not something you can see with the naked eye, but with meditation, practise and prayer, the true nature of the sacredness of all reality unfolds. Contemplate that this is the Sacred Wisdom revealed in the mystical traditions of Moses, Jesus Christ, Mohammed and Buddha.

4 Commit to reanimating your life with recognition of Divine presence.

SHIVA'S DANCE

Meditate on the symbolism of the Hindu god Shiva's Cosmic Dance and understand how the universe works. Contemplate Shiva's dance of Creation, Preservation and Destruction to learn that your world is truly sacred.

Benefits

- Introduces you to the Hindu God Shiva

- Helps you learn from Shiva's qualities

- Helps you shed things that no longer serve you

Shiva is often depicted with four arms dancing in a ring of fire. He is the third god of the Hindu triad made up of Brahma the creator, Vishnu the preserver and Shiva the destroyer. It is the destruction created by Shiva that allows for positive recreation. For example, an artist may melt down old pieces of metal during the process of creating a beautiful new sculpture.

Meditation

When

Try this meditation if you need to shed lacklustre ideas, relationships or activities that no longer serve you well.

Preparation

Find an image of Shiva at your library or on the Web.

Practice

1 Sit on a cushion or chair in your mediation space. Breathe deeply for a few minutes in order to relax and centre your mind.

2 Visualize Shiva dancing in his ring of fire. Contemplate the dynamic quality of life and the importance of destruction in the life cycle. Remember that all life is in constant motion, like Shiva dancing his cosmic dance. Relax into the idea that all is change and nothing is static or fixed.

3 Think of your past and how things you have owned no longer exist as they once were. For instance, you may have owned a car that is now being used for scrap metal. Think of relationships you have had that have ended through death or separation. Recall how new relationships, ideas and realities have entered your life.

4 Think of something – an idea, a job, a relationship or an attitude – you may need to shed. Contemplate Shiva's dance to understand the dynamic quality of your life and to help you 'destroy' that which is no longer positive, in order to 'create' and 'preserve' that which serves you and the universe.

5 End your meditation by visualizing letting go of whatever is no longer serving you.

PERSONAL GOD VS MYSTICAL REALITY

Judaism, Christianity and Islam have each developed the idea of a personal God, which has helped countless believers to mature spiritually as human beings. Yet the idea of a personal God can also encourage you to judge, condemn and justify harm to others.

Benefits

- Helps you avoid religious pitfalls
- Encourages contemplation of your meaning of the Divine
- Promotes spiritual maturity

Each of the three monotheisms listed above developed a mystical tradition that considers God as a symbol of a reality that cannot be described. This meditation helps you explore your understanding of the Divine in your own spiritual path.

Meditation

When

Try this meditation when you want to explore your understanding of the Divine.

Preparation

Write about what the Divine means to you.

Practice

1 Sit on a cushion or chair in your meditation space. Meditate on your breath for five minutes.

2 Bring to mind your understanding of God or the Divine. You may be an atheist, an agnostic, a Buddhist or Hindu. Or you may consider yourself a practitioner of one of the three monotheistic religions mentioned above – Judaism, Christianity or Islam.

3 Is God a symbol for you of mystical realities or a personal God with human qualities like your own? Do you feel you embody 'Divine potential', as in the Buddhist tradition of enlightenment? Or do you feel you are separate from God? Do you feel you can merge with God in prayer? If you don't believe in a personal God, do you have some other form of a higher power, a mystical understanding of reality or another way of understanding the Divine?

4 Do you have any feelings that 'God is on your side' and against others? Do you feel that this is a problem? Is your God a punishing God? If this is so, consider the negative side of this attitude for yourself and others.

5 Continue meditating on these questions for several sessions. Make sure you fully explore your notion of the Divine. There are no right or wrong answers and it is all right to not know precisely what you think. The idea is to ask the questions and answer them as best as you can.

GLOSSARY

AMATERASU Great sun goddess of Japan and supreme deity of the Shinto religion. She is especially worshipped at the Winter Solstice when the sun begins to return for the spring planting.

AVALOKITESHVARA A Tibetan Buddhist deity considered the embodiment of the compassionate nature of all buddhas.

BODHISATTVA A person who has profound compassion who, having already attained enlightenment, postpones his or her entrance into Nirvana in order to help others do the same.

BRAHMA A creator god, the first of the Hindu trinity, often represented with four heads looking to the four corners of the world.

BUDDHA Means literally 'one who has awakened'. Buddha is the enlightened form of Siddhartha Gautama, also know as Shakyamuni, who was born in 563 BCE and was the founder/creator of Buddhism as a spiritual practice. A buddha is also a person who has achieved enlightenment and is free of every kind of craving or negativity.

CHAKRA A Sanskrit word meaning 'wheel'. Both Hindus and Buddhists believe there are seven chakras or subtle energy centres in the body located along the spine, which can be 'opened' through certain physical movements and psychic/mental/spiritual techniques, so that the energy can be released and utilized.

DERVISH A member of a Turkish Sufi Muslim sect who practices a whirling dance to reach religious ecstasy and connection with Allah.

IZANAGI The Japanese Shinto god who fathered the islands and gods of Japan with his sister Izanami.

KABBALAH The Hebrew word 'Kaballah' means to receive and refers to the communication between God and Moses. Kabbalah is a mystical form of the Jewish religion that places emphasis on the symbolism of syllables and numbers.

KIN HIN A form of walking meditation practiced by Zen Buddhists that often breaks long periods of sitting meditation.

KUAN YIN One of the most important and best-loved Chinese Buddhist female deities. She is considered the living expression of compassion, and is also associated with the Tibetan Avalokiteshvara, the Japanese Kwannon and the Tibetan female Buddha Tara.

MALA Buddhist rosary with 108 beads used as an aid for mantra repetition.

MANDALA A circular design that can symbolize the self, the cosmos or the environment of a deity.

MANI Short for 'Om Mani Padme Hum', a famous Tibetan Buddhist Mantra that literally means 'Behold! The Jewel in the Lotus'. It is taught that each syllable purifies the suffering in the six realms of existence. 'Om' purifies pride, 'Ma' jealousy, 'Ni' desire, 'Pa' stupidity, 'Me' possessiveness and 'Hum' hatred.

MANTRA A sacred syllable or sequence of syllables repeated many times in meditation in order to protect the mind from negativity and connect with enlightened existence. One of the most well known is the sacred mantra 'Om'.

MERIDIANS Energy channels in the body that circulate the 'chi' or life energy. Chinese acupuncturists use the 2000 recognized points along the 12 major meridians to insert needles to treat various illnesses.

NIRVANA A Sanskrit word meaning 'extinction' or 'blowing out', referring to the end of suffering and desire. Liberation from the cycle of endless rebirth and suffering; a state of peace.

SAMSARA In Buddhism, the existence of ordinary beings, characterized by constant rebirth in one or another of the six realms of rebirth. Samsara is characterized by suffering and dissatisfaction.

SAVASANA A reclining yoga posture, also called the 'corpse pose' used for deep relaxation.

SHAKTI In the Hindu religion, Shiva's consort; divine female energy. Creative energy perceived as a female deity.

SHIVA Shiva is the destroyer aspect of the Hindu trinity of gods.

SPIDER WOMAN A female deity of the Native American Hopi/Navajo Tribes considered the female force of all creation. She holds all creation together in her web that links everybody and everything.

SUSANOWO Japanese Shinto god of the sea and storms known to have a furious temper. Brother of the Japanese Sun Goddess Amaterasu.

TARA A female bodhisattva of compassion especially venerated by Tibetan Buddhists. She took the vow to actively perpetuate the spread of enlightenment until not a single unenlightened being remained. She further pledged to take rebirth only as a woman until all beings are enlightened.

TINGSHAS Two very small cymbal-shaped discs struck together to produce a ringing sound. Buddhists use tingshas to clear a space of negative energy or to begin and end a meditation session.

TONGLEN Means 'giving and receiving'. In this Tibetan Buddhist practice one breathes in the pain and suffering of others and breathes out love and compassion. The practice is intended to increase the compassion, as well as destroy the selfish ego of the practitioner.

UZUME Japanese Shinto goddess of mirth who lured the sun goddess Amaterasu out of her cave with lewd dancing and bawdy jokes. She is similar to the goddess Baubo in the Western tradition.

VISHNU One of the Hindu trinity of gods, the preserver or caretaker of the universe, who balances everything that exists.

ZABUTON A rectangular cushion designed to go underneath a meditation cushion to protect ankles and knees from a hard floor.

INDEX

E

eating *see* food
Emotional Mind 49, 74–5
Emotional Mindfulness 93, 114–15
Emotional Storm 49, 88–9
EMT (Eye Movement Therapy) 144
ethical decisions 278–9, 284–5
evening meditation 24
exercises, stretching 23, 24–5, 39
Expand your Heart 225, 254–5
experiencing 17
Eye Movement Therapy (EMT) 144
eyes 37, 38
The Eyes Have It 93, 126–7

F

Facing the Mirror 279, 294–5
fear, Tara meditation on 172–3
Fear and Love 225, 252–3
Feed your Demons 136, 146–7
Flower Power 49, 82–3
Flowing Water 49, 62–3
focusing 14–15
Follow your Bliss 305, 328–9
food meditations
  Nourishment 178–9
  Ripe fruit 93, 110–11

A Tasteful Meditation 93, 108–9
For the Highest Good 304, 306–7
Forgiveness 224, 234–5
49 Days 136, 140–1
Four Directions 336, 338–9
Four Immeasurables 224, 236–7
'The Four Noble Truths' 337, 358–9
Four Powers 137, 162–3
Fox, George 348
Francis of Assisi, St 337, 360–1
Free Sentient Beings 224, 238–9

G

Gaynor, Dr Mitchell 70
get moving *see* movement meditation
Get Out of Debt 279, 290–1
Glass Half-full 93, 94–5
Good Birth 137, 160–1
Great Tree meditation 137, 156–7
Greet Your Day 49, 78–9
Gregorian chant 49, 68–9
grief, unresolved 20, 136

H

hand posture 37
healing meditations 9–10, 18, 42,
  135–97

S

T

ACKNOWLEDGEMENTS

AKG, London/Jean-Louis Nou 174. **Bridgeman Art Library, London/New York**/British Museum, London, UK 362. **Corbis UK Ltd**/98, 158, 288, 300, 382; /Alen Macweeney 154; /Ariel Skelley 206; /Arte & Immagini srl 356; /Bob Krist 286; /Charles & Josette Lenars 188; /Christie's Images 354; /David Martinez 209; /Elio Ciol 360; /Franco Vogt 144; /Jose Luis Pelaez 352; /Justin Hutchinson 117; /L. Clarke 170; /NASA 131; /Owen Franken 366; /Richard Cummins 350; /Roy McMahon 84; /Ted Streshinsky 380; /Tom Stewart 124; /W. Wayne Lockwood, M.D. 319; /Yoshitoshi 343. **Eye Ubiquitous** 316. **Getty Images** 38-39, 112, 147, 161, 182, 187, 205, 218, 232, 234, 236, 242, 252, 258, 280, 282, 292, 294, 326, 338, 378; /Adastra 308;/Peter Adams 312; /Daniel Allan 320; /Ty Allison 268; /Paul & Lindamarie Ambrose 88; /Ross Anania 290; /Jim Arbogast 254; /David Ash 330; /Martin Barraud 8; /Nancy

Brown 250; /Buccina Studios 32; /Burke/Triolo Productions 162; /Paul S Conrath 102; /Neil Emmerson 118; /David Epperson 9; /Andrew Errington 128; /Grant Faint 212; /Adam Friedberg 231; /Todd Gipstein 97; /Tim Hall 12; /Jason Hawkes 202; /Gavin Hellier 264; /Hisham F Ibrahim 68-69; /Gavriel Jecan 226; /Michael Krasowitz 192; /John Lamb 217; /Sanna Lindberg 18; /Ghislain & Marie David de Lossy 86; /Manchan 240; /Ebby May 374; /Patti McConville 180; /Ian Mckinnell 72; /Rob Meinychuk 107; /George F Mobley 239; /Jen Petreshock 314; /Jurgen Reisch 260; /Rick Rusing 150; /David Sacks 256; /Ellen Schuster 74; /Stephen Simpson 220; /Jeff Spielman 285; /Szczepaniak 94; /Mequmi Takamura 28; /Alan Thornton 149; /Andrew Bret Wallis 140; /Jeremy Woodhouse 132-133. **Octopus Publishing Group Limited** 2, 4, 6-7, 11, 15, 16, 20-21, 26, 27, 30-31, 33, 34-35, 36 Top, 36 Bottom, 40-41, 43, 51, 52-53, 54, 56, 61, 63, 64, 66, 70, 76-77, 78, 79, 82, 100, 104-105, 108, 111, 114-115, 120, 122, 127, 139, 143, 152, 156, 164, 166, 169, 178, 184, 190, 194-195, 198, 200, 210, 214, 222, 224, 228, 249, 262, 266, 271, 272, 274, 276, 278, 296, 299, 302, 304, 307, 310, 322, 324, 328, 332, 334, 336, 341, 344, 347, 358, 364, 368, 370, 373, 377; /Walter Gardiner 23; /Ian Parsons 1, 14, 29, 58, 348; /Peter Pugh-Cook 244; /Ian Wallace 25, 246. **Science Photo Library**/Garion Hutchings 196. **The Picture Desk Ltd**/The Art Archive/Private Collection Paris/Dagli Orti 176.

Executive Editor Brenda Rosen
Managing Editor Clare Churly
Executive Art Editor Sally Bond
Designer Pia Ingham for Cobalt Id
Picture Library Manager Jennifer Veall
Production Manager Louise Hall